Your First $100k

Your First $100k

The Step-by-Step Path to Building Wealth, Confidence, and Control

Julian Raye

Mindful Pages

Published in 2025

ISBN: 9789371773126 (PB)
ISBN: 9789371774086 (eBook)

Published by

Mindful Pages
Imprint of Alpha Editions LLC
312 W. 2nd St #1834
Casper, WY 82601, USA

This book was developed using advanced writing tools to support the drafting and ideation process. All content has been thoughtfully curated, refined, and reviewed to ensure quality and relevance.

Content

Introduction
This Isn't Just About Money

Let's start with a truth that few financial guides dare to voice: money is never solely about money. It is a question of autonomy. Of power. Of whether you move through life with deliberate choice or constant compromise. Whether your decisions are driven by freedom or fear. The first £100,000 you earn and retain is far more than a numerical milestone—it marks a structural shift in how you relate to the world, and how the world responds to you.

This book will not insult your intelligence with tired advice about skipping lattes or rising at 5 a.m. Nor will it offer gimmicks or a rigid blueprint claiming universality. What it promises instead is far rarer: a framework for thinking about money that aligns your actions with your values, your goals with your psychology, and your daily routines with long-term sovereignty. This is not merely about growing net worth; it is about reclaiming the narrative of your life.

Why the focus on £100k? Because reaching that threshold transforms more than your bank account. It shifts your perception, your decision-making, even your nervous system. Before it, every financial choice feels like a test of endurance; after it, possibilities broaden. You begin to operate in a different register—not scarcity, but leverage, design, and intentional growth.

Yet crossing that threshold is rarely taught. Our institutions, media, and social norms condition us to conflate income with identity, busyness with productivity, ambition with guilt, scarcity with shame. Money is framed as stress or status, rarely as a tool of alignment.

This book addresses those distortions. It is for those weary of reaction—reacting to bills, job offers, family pressures, algorithm-fed aspirations that feel foreign. Whether you start from debt, disillusionment, or digital fatigue, what follows is a path from passivity to authorship. Each chapter equips you not merely with information, but with frameworks for clearer thinking, deliberate action, and a financial life that reflects who you truly are.

We begin by deconstructing the myth that financial success is solely about hard work or luck. It is neither—at least, not entirely. Most of us labour hard; many of us experience fortune and misfortune. What distinguishes those who gain control from those who remain trapped is subtler: the capacity to see money as leverage, not merely a scoreboard. The first £100k is the point where options emerge—not because you've "arrived," but because you've stopped losing ground.

Consider this: earning £30,000 a year but spending £32,000 leaves more than a £2,000 deficit. It places you psychologically underwater. Every unexpected expense feels existential; long-term planning collapses. As you approach your first £100k in savings, investments, or working capital, your mindset begins to shift. You move from panic to pattern, from scarcity to possibility.

This shift is cultural as much as practical. In a society still structured around compliance and consumption, building your first £100k is an act of quiet defiance. It declares: I will not wait to be rescued. I will not outsource my choices. I will not contort myself to fit a story that keeps me small.

Yet this is not a manifesto for martyrdom or relentless grind. It is not about glorifying deprivation or frugality. Instead, it invites deliberate action: spending with awareness, investing with context, earning in ways that preserve your integrity. Wealth, framed thus, becomes a tool—a means to design a life that aligns with your values.

The chapters ahead build cumulatively. Chapter One examines why the first £100k carries disproportionate psychological weight. It is not about lifestyle acquisition; it is about identity transformation. You begin to see yourself as someone who builds, decides, and owns. We explore the shift from scarcity loops to strategic thinking, and confront the emotional cost of delayed action—the opportunities lost not only in money, but in self-trust.

Chapter Two addresses a pervasive trap: conflating income with identity. Too many internalise job prestige or low pay as measures of intrinsic worth. We separate earning power from ego, and explore decentralised, modern pathways to income that bypass outdated hierarchies and linear careers.

Chapter Three reframes spending—not as budgeting, but as a lens into belief systems. Every pound spent reflects what you consider worthy of investment. We guide you to audit not just transactions, but underlying narratives, and distinguish sustainable joy from ephemeral dopamine.

Debt takes centre stage in Chapter Four. Rather than moralising, we unpack the psychological contracts debt represents and offer actionable, customised exit strategies. Escaping debt is not merely arithmetic; it is story editing—reclaiming narrative control alongside fiscal stability.

Chapter Five shifts from survival to systems. Willpower is unreliable; structure is liberating. Tools such as the three-account framework and the anti-budget are introduced to create a financial operating system that aligns with your psychology rather than works against it.

Chapter Six explores income stacking. Beyond trading hours for money, we examine ways to build assets that earn in your absence: digital products, licensing, creative leverage, or small-scale ventures. Here, the focus is finding your unique point of advantage while rejecting the myth that more hours equate to more success.

Investing is demystified in Chapter Seven. Stripped of jargon and intimidation, investing is framed not as gambling, but as a non-negotiable act of expansion. Saving protects; investing grows. Both are essential for long-term autonomy.

Chapter Eight reframes money as a relationship, not a religion. Emotional entanglements that distort decisions are examined, with practices offered for honest, healthy conversations—both with yourself and others. Readers craft personal "money vows," principles that transcend individual paychecks or purchases.

Finally, Chapter Nine zooms out. With foundational control established, we ask: what is your financial life ultimately for? Wealth's utility lies in enabling intentional design. We explore reverse-engineering the life you desire—geographically, professionally, socially—and making long-term bets that yield freedom, not merely funds.

By the book's end, your finances may transform—but so too will your sense of self. The objective is not escape through wealth, but engagement on your own terms. Not performance, but embodiment: resilient, sovereign, and quietly intentional.

The first £100k is not a finish line. It is proof of concept: that structure can emerge from chaos, that earning, growth, and alignment are possible even in a system not built for your flourishing. Most importantly, it signals a shift—from reactive to proactive, from consumer to creator, from uncertain to unshakeable.

You are not here to hustle harder. You are here to build wiser. Let's begin.

Chapter 1
Why $100k Changes Everything

There is a reason seasoned investors, veteran entrepreneurs, and even economists speak of the first £100,000 with a peculiar reverence. Not because it is, by contemporary standards, an immense fortune—indeed, in an era of inflation and global volatility, it scarcely buys luxury or guarantees retirement. Yet ask anyone who has built it from scratch, especially without inherited wealth, and a familiar sentiment emerges: the first £100k feels uniquely arduous, psychologically defining in ways that subsequent six-figure milestones rarely match. It signals the shift from theory to proof, from merely surviving to manoeuvring, from dreaming to designing. Think of it as oxygen at altitude—the difference between gasping and gaining height.

To grasp why this particular sum carries such disproportionate influence, we must peer beneath spreadsheets and interest rates. This chapter is less about mechanics—how to earn, save, or invest—and more about the mental architecture required to arrive there. That architecture begins with perception: how you gauge your own potential, confront risk, and calculate possibility. Your relationship to this milestone is shaped not by numbers alone, but by narrative—both the inherited story and the one you are positioned to author.

The psychological heft of £100k derives partly from what it represents: accumulated proof. For those who have not experienced the transition, the difference can be hard to articulate. Before reaching it, money feels abstract—something to chase, to avoid, or to monitor with anxiety. After, it becomes a material you can shape, a resource with agency rather than a torrent slipping through your fingers. And agency, as ever, holds more power than acquisition.

The shift is neither linear nor purely rational. Behavioural economists remind us that financial choices are largely emotional, often subconscious. Fear, status pressure, learned helplessness, cultural mimicry—these exert more influence than models or projections. Attaining £100k requires more than knowledge or discipline; it requires transformation of habits and identity alike.

Early financial life is dominated for many by scarcity loops—neurological patterns reinforced by stress, anxiety, and the chronic sense of insufficiency. In scarcity mode, everything is urgent: rent, minimum payments, grocery stretch. Planning becomes a luxury. Energy is consumed by reaction, leaving scant capacity for long-term strategy. In this context, even imagining £100k can feel absurd—like asking someone in drought to design an irrigation system.

And yet, the loop is breakable—not instantly, not without friction. The key is not brute force through willpower, but a shift in perception. Capital is a tool: a buffer, a lever, a multiplier of decision-making. With a few thousand saved, choices begin to change. Ten thousand allows professional experimentation; fifty thousand supports calculated risk-taking. At £100k, posture transforms from defensive to proactive, from constraint to consideration. The question shifts: from "How do I get by?" to "What might I build, given trust in my footing?"

Cultivating that trust is no small feat in a culture that distorts money into a moral mirror. Status, self-worth, financial image—they are entwined deliberately. Spend more, and you appear successful; earn less, and you are subtly marked as insufficient. This "money mirror" reflects not your reality, but external valuation.

For this reason, it is essential to interrogate what £100k means to you—not peers, bosses, or influencers, but your own sense of security, potential, and self-definition. Stripped of social signalling, £100k is a psychological inflection point: the threshold at which long-term strategy becomes viable, and identity can detach from survival to align with growth.

Confronting internal scripts is equally critical. Inherited beliefs—often subtle and unexamined—shape what we perceive as permissible to earn or save. For some, wealth implies greed or betrayal; for others, it conflicts with creativity, integrity, or simplicity. These scripts are neither universal nor trivial; they constrain possibility. Believing, even unconsciously, that success diminishes worth or alienates community subtly sabotages ascent.

Thus, we begin here: with terrain, not tactics. Building £100k sustainably demands psychological groundwork. You must reconcile ambition with self-conception, decouple worth from current income, and treat financial decisions as evidence of a future story rather than isolated transactions.

The cost of delay is rarely captured in spreadsheets: opportunity lost, confidence deferred. Every year spent waiting compounds uncertainty; each month of prioritising short-term survival entrenches habituated reaction. The first £100k is transformative not merely because of growth, but because it shifts you—from passive to active, from reactive to designer.

Consider two individuals with similar earnings. One consistently saves, monitors spending, and invests in low-fee index funds; the other waits for raises, readiness, or debt clearance. Five years later, the first has cultivated a financial cushion and a mindset of clarity and autonomy. The second may earn slightly more but remains psychologically exposed, still reacting, still waiting. The divergence is directional as much as numerical: one acts from stability, the other from strain.

The first £100k is a behavioural turning point. It requires different thinking, different habits, different self-belief. It invites a new mode: structure over hustle, awareness over anxiety, design over default. The money matters—but what it awakens within you endures.

In the chapters ahead, we will explore these dimensions: breaking scarcity loops, interrogating wealth and worth, and rewriting the narratives governing your financial beliefs. We will quantify the real cost of delay—not merely pounds lost, but proof deferred. And we will build a foundation for financial authorship: the capacity to script, sculpt, and sustain a life where money serves, rather than constrains.

Once you have built your first £100k, guesswork fades. You no longer hope that things "just work out." You possess evidence, leverage, strategy—and perhaps most profoundly, a new lens: not as someone striving to get ahead, but as someone who already is.

The Psychology of a Milestone

At first glance, £100,000 is just a number—an arbitrary figure on a bank statement, or a milestone repeated so often in financial advice that it begins to feel cliché. But for those who have reached it without inheritance or windfall, the first £100k carries a psychological weight that far exceeds its numerical value. It marks a line—between theory and proof, instability and traction, guessing and knowing. What makes it powerful is not the purchasing power alone, but what it begins to do to your inner architecture: your beliefs, behaviours, and sense of self-direction.

There is something qualitatively different about building the first £100k compared to any financial milestone that follows. Once you cross this threshold, you don't merely have money—you have evidence. You've internalised that your actions, when structured and sustained, can produce significant results. And that shift—from financial abstraction to financial authorship—is more profound than compound interest or market returns. It reshapes your sense of what's possible. The first £100k is a psychological inflection point because it transforms the *kind of person you believe yourself to be.*

Behavioural economists have long explored the disconnect between how people *should* behave around money and how they *actually* do. Traditional financial theory, grounded in the assumption of rational actors, collapses under the reality that most people are emotionally and behaviourally inconsistent with their own stated goals. The gap is not just a knowledge gap—it's a psychological one. Money is entangled with identity, safety, status, and control. And until you accumulate a meaningful financial cushion, that entanglement governs your decisions more than any spreadsheet ever could.

One of the most unspoken aspects of building wealth—especially from zero or below—is the way your internal perception of risk evolves as your resources increase. When you're operating with nothing but a paycheque and perhaps a few hundred pounds of discretionary cash, the concept of risk is distorted. It doesn't function rationally. You avoid small risks that could bring long-term gain (like investing or switching careers) because even minor volatility feels existential. Conversely, you may take on destructive risks—overusing credit, ignoring contracts, overworking without return—because you feel cornered and desperate for a breakthrough. In both cases, the problem isn't that you're irrational. It's that your margin for error is so narrow that rationality can't function.

Reaching £100k starts to change that dynamic. It widens the margin. With savings or investments behind you, your tolerance for *intelligent* risk increases. You can afford to think in horizons rather than pay cycles. You don't overreact to a surprise bill or a slow month. Crucially, you begin to experience what psychologists call *self-efficacy*: the belief that your actions lead to predictable and meaningful outcomes. That belief is a cornerstone of personal agency. And in the financial domain, it doesn't come from reading theory—it comes from practice and accumulation.

Much of early financial behaviour is driven not by planning, but by pattern repetition—what might be called *scarcity conditioning*. If you've grown up in a household where money was always tight, where bills were juggled and financial fear hovered in the background, then your brain has likely learned to associate money with stress. Neuroscience backs this up: chronic financial stress has a measurable impact on cognitive bandwidth, executive function, and even memory. In one well-cited Princeton study, researchers found that financial insecurity could lower cognitive performance by as much as 13 IQ points—the equivalent of losing a full night's sleep. Under those conditions, thinking strategically is not a matter of effort, but of physiological limitation.

The scarcity loop is not simply a product of low income—it's a feedback mechanism. You feel uncertain about money, so you avoid financial decisions. That avoidance creates disorganisation or inaction, which leads to poor outcomes, which in turn reinforces the original uncertainty. The result is not just financial stasis, but psychological paralysis. The first £100k interrupts this loop. It doesn't eliminate fear entirely, but it alters your *reference point.* You no longer make decisions from the edge of panic. You operate with breathing room. And from that breathing room, clarity becomes possible.

The cultural context only amplifies these dynamics. We are bombarded daily with images of extreme wealth, curated lifestyles, and algorithmic aspiration. In that environment, £100k can feel both trivial and unattainable. Trivial, because it doesn't match the fantasy wealth of celebrity and tech culture. Unattainable, because for many, even the first thousand feels like a miracle. But part of the psychological power of the first £100k is that it *grounds* you. It is a meaningful target that is both ambitious and achievable. It is large enough to require structure and strategy, but not so far away that it collapses under the weight of abstraction.

This is especially true when you consider what £100k represents across contexts. It may be the seed of a house deposit, the foundation for entrepreneurship, the buffer that lets you walk away from an exploitative job, or simply the removal of background noise—an end to constant worry. In each case, the number is not the point. The shift in psychological posture is. When you cross that threshold, you stop making decisions solely based on what you can afford *today*. You start making them based on what you want to build *next*.

There is also a deeper, subtler transformation that accompanies this milestone: a reframing of identity. For many, money has always been externally defined—what others earn, what others expect, what status you are supposed to perform. But building £100k from intentional choices forces you to become financially self-referential. You begin to see your own patterns, your own values, your own tempo. That kind of self-awareness is rare in the financial world, which often revolves around either shame or spectacle. But it is foundational if you are to build sustainable wealth, not just superficial income.

Importantly, this transformation is not only personal—it is relational. Your posture in social, professional, and family contexts shifts subtly but significantly. You may find yourself less reactive in financial conversations, less envious of others' success, more curious about long-term decisions rather than short-term validation. These changes are rarely dramatic. But they are cumulative. And they are stabilising.

At this point, some will argue that money should not be tied to self-worth—that using a financial milestone as a psychological marker is dangerous or reductive. And in abstract terms, they're right. Worth is intrinsic. Money does not measure character. But in the lived experience of economic systems, money does measure *access*. It influences time, safety, and optionality. And to pretend otherwise is to ignore the material conditions that govern much of adult life. The goal is not to conflate wealth with worth, but to recognise that your relationship with money is inseparable from how you move through the world. To change that relationship is not to moralise money, but to *depower* it—so that it no longer owns your narrative.

There is also the often-ignored issue of delayed action. Too many people lose years waiting for the perfect moment: to earn more, to feel ready, to have it all figured out. But the real cost of that delay is not just lost returns or missed opportunities. It's lost *confidence*. Every year spent without movement reinforces the belief that movement is not possible. Every financial decision deferred becomes a silent vote against your own capability. By contrast, every step towards £100k—however small—becomes a reinforcing loop of self-trust.

You are not just earning more or saving better. You are becoming someone who *follows through.*

It is worth noting, too, that while subsequent financial milestones may be larger, they rarely feel as transformational. Once you've built £100k, building the next comes with experience, systems, and leverage. But the first requires something else entirely. It requires you to learn financial structure from scratch, to withstand setbacks without losing momentum, and to act consistently in the absence of immediate validation. It requires resilience without glamour, and persistence without applause.

And so, this milestone matters—not because £100k is a magical figure, but because it reflects something that cannot be given, borrowed, or taught: *internal authority.* It marks the point at which your financial life stops being an emergency and starts becoming a strategy. It is not a destination, but a foundation. Not a finish line, but a shift in gravitational pull—from drifting to directing.

When you build your first £100k, you are not simply accumulating capital. You are accumulating *evidence*—that your choices create results, that your patterns can evolve, and that your future can be shaped, not merely endured. And once you have that evidence, everything else becomes easier to believe.

From Scarcity Loops to Strategic Thinking

Scarcity does more than limit what you can afford—it distorts how you think. When resources are scarce, time becomes compressed, decisions become reactive, and imagination begins to shrink. You stop planning for the future and start triaging the present. From the outside, this looks like irresponsibility or shortsightedness. But from the inside, it's a relentless calculus: *What can I get away with delaying? What can I juggle? What's the least-worst option available to me today?* The loop is not a character flaw. It is a neurological and behavioural response to prolonged uncertainty.

This dynamic has been studied across disciplines—behavioural economics, psychology, neuroscience—and the findings converge: chronic financial stress impairs cognitive functioning. In the groundbreaking work of Sendhil Mullainathan and Eldar Shafir, for example, scarcity was shown to reduce mental bandwidth, compromise problem-solving, and increase impulsivity. Not because individuals are less intelligent or motivated, but because the cognitive load of scarcity taxes the brain's executive functions. This matters because the skills most needed for wealth-building—planning, delayed gratification, abstraction, foresight—are precisely the ones that become harder to access when you're constantly navigating shortage.

The result is a behavioural trap. You make short-term decisions not out of laziness or ignorance, but because your mind is consumed with survival. Pay the late fee now or skip groceries? Take the predatory loan or lose housing? Stay in the dead-end job because you can't risk two unpaid weeks? These are not strategic questions. They are defensive ones. And over time, they create a behavioural groove—a loop—where long-term vision atrophies and reaction becomes the default mode of engagement.

Breaking that loop is not as simple as cutting expenses or increasing income, though both are often necessary. The deeper task is psychological: shifting from a state of threat management to one of deliberate planning. This shift is not immediate. It requires a slow recalibration of internal signals—a reconditioning of your nervous system to stop treating money as a crisis trigger and start treating it as a planning tool.

One of the first symptoms that you're escaping the scarcity loop is a change in time perception. You stop counting in days and weeks and start thinking in months and years. This shift in time orientation is not superficial. It reflects a core transformation in how you relate to both risk and reward. You begin to see the benefits of investing in something that won't pay off tomorrow. You develop what psychologists call *future orientation*: the capacity to act in the present based on anticipated future states. This is a defining feature of strategic thinkers across disciplines—from elite athletes to successful entrepreneurs to long-term investors.

But future orientation requires *trust*—in your own stability, in the persistence of your environment, and in the reliability of your choices. And trust is not easily cultivated when your past financial life has been marked by volatility or precarity. Many people struggle to plan not because they lack discipline, but because every prior attempt to plan has been interrupted by crisis. They've learned, often unconsciously, that it's safer to stay reactive than to hope, only to be destabilised again. This is where the work of rebuilding begins—not with spreadsheets, but with narrative repair.

To move from scarcity to strategy, you have to begin by interrogating the story you've internalised about control. Do you believe that your financial outcomes are primarily determined by your choices, or by external forces? This distinction—known in psychology as *locus of control*—matters profoundly. Those with an external locus tend to feel helpless, victimised by circumstances, and disengaged from planning. Those with an internal locus, by contrast, feel empowered to influence outcomes through effort and structure. Shifting from external to internal doesn't mean denying systemic challenges—it means reclaiming agency where it *does* exist, however modestly at first.

Consider the difference between someone who says, "I can't save because I don't earn enough," and someone who says, "I haven't yet designed a system that makes saving automatic, even on a small scale." The first statement closes the door on strategy. The second opens a line of inquiry. Strategic thinking begins with such reframes—not toxic positivity, but constructive possibility. It asks: *Given my current constraints, what variables can I influence? What can I prototype, test, or systematise, even in miniature?*

This is where structure enters. Scarcity loops are often accompanied by chaos—no budget, no tracking, no systematised review. Money comes in, money goes out, and nothing is measured or mapped. Strategic thinking, by contrast, depends on *externalising cognition*. This means getting the information out of your head and into visible systems: a calendar, a ledger, a visual tracker, a planning tool. Externalising reduces the mental load and increases feedback accuracy. You stop relying on hunches and start relying on patterns. You stop reacting to stress and start designing for resilience.

Crucially, strategic thinking is *not* the same as perfectionism. In fact, perfectionism can be its enemy. Many people stay stuck in scarcity loops because they think financial organisation must be total, perfect, and aesthetically polished to be effective. So they wait until they feel ready to go all in. But strategy doesn't require readiness—it requires movement. It's far better to have a rough plan executed with consistency than a perfect plan deferred indefinitely. Strategy is iterative. It gets refined through action.

Another vital shift occurs in your relationship with failure. In scarcity loops, mistakes feel catastrophic. A missed payment, an unexpected bill, a declined card—each becomes a psychological blow, reinforcing a narrative of inadequacy or futility. In strategic thinking, mistakes are data. They reveal system flaws, behavioural tendencies, or environmental blind spots. This shift requires emotional regulation and perspective, but it pays dividends. You become less fragile and more adaptive. You stop internalising setbacks as proof of failure and start treating them as inputs for better models.

To illustrate this, take the example of someone who sets out to build an emergency fund. From a scarcity perspective, every month where savings fall short is a failure, a confirmation that they're "bad with money." From a strategic perspective, each month is feedback: Was the savings goal realistic? Were fixed costs accurately estimated? Did unexpected expenses reveal a gap in planning? Strategic thinking doesn't mean avoiding mistakes—it means *extracting insight* from them.

This brings us to a deeper truth: scarcity loops are not just financial patterns—they are emotional ecosystems. They are shaped by shame, fear, self-judgment, and sometimes unprocessed trauma. Escaping the loop requires emotional intelligence as much as financial knowledge. It involves cultivating psychological distance from your numbers—learning to observe them without collapse, to make decisions without panic, to take action without over-identifying with every fluctuation. Emotional detachment is not indifference—it's clarity. It's the ability to hold your finances in your hands, not in your chest.

Over time, this clarity builds momentum. You begin to notice a reduction in financial friction—fewer surprises, smoother processes, more predictable outcomes. You don't get caught in the same cycles. You anticipate. You buffer. You act before you're forced to react. These are small victories, often invisible to others, but profoundly meaningful. Because each one represents a new reference point—a shift from surviving to steering.

The final layer of this transition involves value alignment. Strategic thinking is not just about efficiency—it's about direction. Once you are no longer consumed by immediate constraints, you can start asking deeper questions: *What do I want money to do for me? What kind of life am I trying to build? What trade-offs am I willing to accept, and which am I no longer willing to make?* These are not abstract reflections. They are strategic imperatives. Because without direction, even well-structured finances can become hollow—a form of wealth accumulation that feels inert, disconnected from purpose.

In this way, the exit from scarcity is not merely a personal upgrade—it is a philosophical one. It requires you to become the kind of person who moves deliberately, who responds to data over fear, and who designs a life rather than drifts through one. It is not a quick shift. It is a gradual rewiring. But once it takes hold, the difference is unmistakable.

You no longer live in constant reaction. You live in response to a plan. A plan you authored. A plan that adjusts, refines, and strengthens with each cycle—not because you've escaped difficulty altogether, but because you've exited the reactive loop that once held you captive. That is the real victory—not wealth alone, but the regained capacity to *think* like someone who builds it.

Status, Self-Worth, and the Money Mirror

Money is often framed as neutral—mere arithmetic, a matter of inputs and outputs, a tool for transactions. But in lived experience, money is almost never just maths. It acts as a mirror: reflecting not only what you have, but what you believe you are worth, what you think is possible, and where you think you belong in the social order. That reflection is not always accurate. More often, it is a composite image—shaped by childhood messages, media saturation, systemic inequalities, peer comparison, and internalised shame. And if left unexamined, that distorted reflection becomes your ceiling.

At the centre of this issue is the culturally reinforced conflation between money and value—not economic value, but personal worth. This conflation is subtle but powerful. From a young age, we are taught to associate financial success with competence, respect, and desirability. School performance is rewarded with praise that implies economic outcomes. Career choices are evaluated based on earning potential. Entire sectors—creative arts, care work, teaching—are framed as "less than" because they pay less, regardless of their social impact. The message is absorbed early: your value is correlated with your financial output.

This social equation is enforced not only by institutions but also by the soft architecture of everyday life—what sociologists call *status signals*. These are the clothes people wear, the devices they carry, the cars they drive, the holidays they post. In theory, we know that such signals are performative. In practice, we internalise them. You see someone earning more, spending more, or investing earlier, and you begin to wonder not just how they did it—but what they know, or are, that you're not. Without conscious resistance, that line of thought quickly becomes corrosive. *If I had their confidence, I'd invest too. If I had their talent, I'd leave this job. If I had their connections, I'd start the business.* What starts as comparison ends as quiet resignation.

This phenomenon has a name: *status anxiety*. Philosopher Alain de Botton wrote at length on its corrosive impact in a society where personal achievement is publicly ranked and privately internalised. In a system where success is visible and failures are hidden, individuals naturally begin to equate money with merit. But that equation breaks down under scrutiny. Wealth, especially in its early stages, is rarely the product of merit alone. It's shaped by access, timing, exposure, luck, and yes, skill—but skill alone is rarely sufficient. When these variables are ignored, people who are under-earning or under-saving begin to see their situation as a reflection of character, rather than circumstance and solvable constraints.

The result is a self-limiting narrative—one that quietly governs financial decisions. A person who sees themselves as someone who "just isn't good with money" will subconsciously avoid engaging with finances at all. Someone who has internalised the belief that people like them "don't become wealthy" will unconsciously resist behaviours that could lead to financial growth—like negotiating salary, investing, or pursuing higher-leverage opportunities. And these beliefs are remarkably resistant to logic. They are not corrected by information; they are reinforced by emotional experience.

Consider, for example, the role of childhood modelling. If you grew up in a household where money was a source of tension, unpredictability, or control, your brain may have coded financial engagement as unsafe. This encoding often persists into adulthood. You may feel a physical discomfort when opening a bank statement or discussing money with a partner. You may sabotage savings progress after a windfall, because having money feels unfamiliar or unearned. These reactions are not about incompetence—they are about identity protection. If you've unconsciously equated financial engagement with threat or shame, avoiding it becomes a form of psychological self-defence.

This is what makes the money mirror so powerful: it reflects more than reality—it reflects belief. And belief, as psychologists have shown time and again, drives behaviour more powerfully than data. If you believe you are someone who can grow, who can learn financial literacy, who can recover from setbacks and build upward mobility, you behave differently. You seek out knowledge. You ask better questions. You take calculated risks. If you believe the opposite, you play small, stay silent, and settle—often without realising it.

To shift this dynamic, the task is not simply financial education—it is *narrative reconstruction.* You must begin to examine the stories you carry about money and identity and ask, with rigour: *Who gave me this belief? What evidence have I collected that contradicts it? What would I do differently if I no longer believed it was true?* These are not easy questions. But they are necessary. Because without conscious rewiring, you remain trapped inside someone else's story—perhaps a parent's fear, a teacher's limitation, a society's prejudice—and mistake it for your own financial reality.

This is especially relevant in contexts of social mobility. First-generation wealth builders often carry a complex emotional burden: pride for what they've achieved, but guilt for leaving behind familiar norms. Their financial growth feels fragile, not because their numbers are weak, but because their sense of belonging is tenuous. They may downplay success to remain relatable. They may underinvest in themselves to avoid accusations of greed or disloyalty. Cultural loyalty can create a psychological tax that limits financial expansion—not because of external resistance, but because of internal conflict.

The mirror also distorts in the other direction. High earners are not immune to self-worth issues—they simply express them differently. Instead of shame about not having enough, there is often fear about losing what they have. Status becomes a cage, performance becomes a defence mechanism, and financial decisions are driven less by utility and more by the need to maintain appearances. Many professionals earning six figures are still living in financial anxiety—not because they are at risk of homelessness, but because their self-worth is so entangled with maintaining a certain lifestyle that every deviation feels existential. This is not a commentary on extravagance—it is a reflection of how deep the identity-money nexus runs.

So, what breaks the cycle? Not disavowal of money, and not blind pursuit of it either. What breaks the cycle is *integration*—the act of separating your worth from your wealth, while still engaging with money strategically and intentionally. This is where tools become important, not just to change outcomes, but to retrain perception. Practices like tracking net worth over time, rather than obsessing over income month to month, can help shift the focus from volatility to progress. Designing financial goals around personal values—not external benchmarks—can reinforce internal motivation. Even simple acts, like automating savings or setting rules-based spending systems, serve a dual purpose: they optimise outcomes and signal to your brain that you are someone who takes money seriously, not fearfully.

But perhaps the most powerful tool is *language*. The words we use to describe our financial lives shape our emotional relationship with them. Replacing "I'm bad with money" with "I'm building a new relationship with money" might sound trivial, but linguistically it repositions you from deficit to agency. Reframing "I can't afford that" to "That's not a priority right now" reasserts choice over lack. These shifts are not about delusion—they are about alignment. They train your internal dialogue to reflect possibility, not paralysis.

Ultimately, the money mirror is not going away. Every day, you will continue to encounter signals—social, digital, familial—that try to reflect back who you are supposed to be financially. But you now have the option to hold your own frame. To decide that your self-worth is not pegged to net worth. To recognise that your potential is not confined to the script you were handed. And to understand, perhaps for the first time, that how you *see* yourself financially may be the most valuable asset you own.

Because once the mirror reflects clarity rather than distortion, your decisions change. You stop overcompensating, underestimating, or avoiding. You begin to act—not from status hunger, shame, or survival—but from alignment. And from there, your financial ceiling is no longer defined by the stories you inherited, but by the strategy you design.

The Real Cost of Waiting

Time is not neutral. It is the silent multiplier behind every financial decision—or indecision. The temptation to wait, to delay action until the conditions feel perfect, is perhaps the most common and costly mistake in wealth-building. It is rarely framed this way, because the cost of inaction is less visible than the cost of mistakes. You can measure a bad investment. You can regret a missed opportunity. But the compounding effect of delayed action—what was *never* started, never earned, never grown—remains invisible. Yet its impact is profound. What appears as caution or procrastination is often an unexamined drain on both wealth and confidence. The real cost of waiting is not just financial; it is psychological, behavioural, and directional.

The numbers themselves are startling. Consider a modest monthly investment of £300. If you begin at age 25 and earn an average annual return of 7%—a historically conservative estimate for broad index-based investments—you'll have over £750,000 by the time you're 65. If you wait just ten years and begin at 35, investing the same amount with the same return, the result drops to roughly £370,000. That decade of hesitation cuts your final outcome by more than half. The lesson here is not about aggression or urgency—it is about compound growth and its dependence on time. The earlier you begin, even with modest amounts, the more powerful your capital becomes. Conversely, the longer you defer action, the more you have to compensate later—either by increasing contributions dramatically or lowering your expectations.

But compound interest is not just a mathematical curiosity. It reflects a broader principle: *that small actions taken early have disproportionately large effects over time.* This applies not only to investments, but to skills, systems, relationships, and habits. The delay in building financial structure—such as automating savings, learning to invest, or switching to a higher-leverage career path—has ripple effects that extend well beyond the next year or two. It shapes your trajectory. It determines what doors will be open to you five or ten years from now.

The psychological dimension of delay is just as critical. Every time you tell yourself, *I'll deal with this later,* you reinforce a subtle belief that you are not yet ready to engage with money in a meaningful way. That belief compounds too. It erodes your sense of agency. You start to identify as someone who avoids complexity, who's always catching up, who watches others act while remaining on the sidelines. Over time, this breeds what behavioural scientists call *learned helplessness*—a passive resignation that conditions you to expect inertia, even when options exist.

What makes this even more challenging is that delayed financial action often masquerades as prudence. People tell themselves they are waiting to "do it properly," to "get all the information," or to "start once they're earning more." But these justifications, while rational on the surface, frequently conceal something deeper: fear of imperfection, fear of making the wrong move, or fear of confronting uncomfortable truths. This is not unique to money. It is a pattern found in every domain where the stakes feel personal—health, relationships, creative work. Yet in finance, the consequences of that fear are often exacerbated by the irreversible nature of time. You cannot retroactively invest at 25 when you're 45. The window doesn't reopen.

Case examples make this dynamic concrete. Take two individuals, both earning £40,000 annually in their late twenties. One begins saving and investing 15% of their income consistently, even during volatile periods. The other waits—first for a raise, then for the economy to feel more stable, then for more "confidence." By their mid-thirties, the difference in outcomes is not just numerical—it's behavioural. The first has developed systems, seen the emotional highs and lows of investing, and built self-trust through action. The second has read extensively, understands the theory, but has no track record. When opportunities arise—buying property, launching a business, relocating—the first feels equipped to assess and act. The second hesitates, unsure of their footing. The gap is no longer just about money. It's about capacity.

This is the real cost of waiting: it doesn't merely stall your wealth—it erodes your momentum. You remain conceptually interested in growth, but structurally unprepared. This matters, because wealth-building is not a single, high-stakes event. It is the cumulative result of repeated, adaptive choices. If those choices are consistently deferred, you don't simply fall behind—you recalibrate your expectations downward. You begin to believe that meaningful wealth is for other people—those who started earlier, those with better luck, those with "a head for money."

There is also an opportunity cost in confidence. Every time you act, even imperfectly, you collect data. You learn how you respond to volatility. You observe your tendencies. You build internal references that guide future decisions. This experiential learning cannot be substituted by research alone. You can read dozens of books on investing and still panic during a market dip—unless you've experienced one with your own money at stake. Confidence is built not by waiting for certainty, but by moving through uncertainty and surviving it. The longer you delay, the more alien the process becomes. And the more foreign it feels, the harder it is to begin.

This creates a paradox: the people most paralysed by financial inaction are often those who most need the psychological upside of early movement. A modest investment, a basic savings system, a low-risk side project—all of these can become symbolic wins. They represent self-direction. They break the pattern of passivity. They generate small but meaningful shifts in how you see yourself. You are no longer someone who's "thinking about it." You are someone who is *doing*, and that identity upgrade is often more valuable than the initial return.

One reason people underestimate the cost of waiting is that modern culture obscures the impact of early financial habits. Digital media is saturated with stories of rapid success—entrepreneurs raising millions, crypto traders striking gold, influencers monetising audiences overnight. Against this backdrop, steady progress feels antiquated. Why invest slowly over ten years when someone on your feed just tripled their net worth last month? This illusion breeds further delay. You tell yourself you need a big idea, a better plan, or more perfect timing. But real wealth, for most people, is not explosive. It is iterative. It is not built on breakthroughs, but on behavioural consistency.

There is a psychological seduction in believing that future-you will handle it. That next year you'll be more disciplined, more informed, more confident. But future-you is a projection. It does not exist independently of your current actions. You become that person not through waiting, but through *earning* their competencies over time. The realisation here is both humbling and empowering: *you don't get readiness first and then act—you act, and readiness emerges through repetition.*

This is why modest beginnings matter so much. You do not need to master investing to open a basic index fund account. You do not need a flawless budget to automate a weekly transfer. You do not need full clarity to block off one hour a week to assess your finances. What you need is the habit of engagement. Once engagement becomes consistent, learning accelerates. Options multiply. You begin to notice opportunities that were previously invisible—not because they weren't there, but because you weren't trained to see them.

It's worth emphasising that waiting is not always a conscious choice. Some people are immobilised by shame, others by complexity, and many by fatigue. Especially for those who have experienced economic trauma—job loss, debt spirals, or generational scarcity—taking control of money can trigger deeply uncomfortable emotions. But this is precisely why early action matters. It creates proof that the loop is breakable. That financial life does not have to be defined by reaction or repair. That momentum is available to those who are willing to act before they feel fully ready.

If you're looking for a clear benchmark, it's this: *any week in which you engage meaningfully with your financial life is a win.* Engagement can mean saving, reviewing expenses, learning a concept, testing a tool, asking a question. What matters is that you are not deferring ownership to a future version of yourself who never arrives. Ownership happens now, in increments. And the cost of delay, while invisible today, will be paid in the form of diminished options later.

There is one final dimension worth naming: regret. People rarely regret early, modest financial action. They may wish they had done it differently, or smarter, but they rarely regret *starting.* What they do regret—often deeply—is the time lost to overthinking, to avoidance, to fear. That regret is corrosive because it is anchored not in failure, but in *non-experience.* There is no data to learn from. No lesson. Just silence where action might have been.

The real cost of waiting, then, is not just lost growth—it is lost authorship. Every month you defer is a month in which you could have been building systems, stacking confidence, gaining insight, and shaping the future in a direction you control. Waiting feels safe, but it is often the riskiest move of all—because while you wait, time compounds on someone else's behalf.

Chapter 2
Income Is Not Identity

At some point in early adulthood—often between the closing years of formal education and the first decade of professional life—a subtle but consequential confusion takes root. What you do begins to stand in for who you are. The job title on a business card, the salary figure on a payslip, the way you describe your work at social gatherings—all start to serve as proxies for identity. When that happens, income stops being merely a tool and quietly becomes a measure of self-worth. The change is almost imperceptible, socially sanctioned, yet profoundly shaping. This chapter begins with a necessary disentangling: your income is not your worth. It never was. If that distinction is not made—and actively defended—it will silently script your financial decisions, emotional reactions, and professional confidence for years to come.

There is a logic to this fusion between income and identity, deeply embedded in capitalist culture. Work functions not only as a means of livelihood but as the scaffolding around status, self-esteem, and moral credibility. A six-figure earner is perceived not simply as wealthier, but as more competent, ambitious, and responsible. These are values projected onto earnings rather than neutral observations. Consequently, earning less can feel like invisibility, or worse, inadequacy. The tension is especially pronounced among knowledge workers, creatives, and service professionals—fields where skill and effort often diverge from income, yet social comparison persists relentlessly.

Modern work culture compounds the issue with linguistic shorthand. "What do you do?" often functions as a subtle inquiry into "Who are you?" LinkedIn profiles collapse personality, history, and trajectory into job summaries. Algorithms prioritise titles, affiliations, and salary bands as markers of relevance or credibility. This is rarely malicious, yet it produces a feedback loop in which income metrics gradually supplant deeper indicators of purpose, alignment, and lived experience.

The danger is not merely psychological. When income becomes identity, financial decisions become distorted. People linger in roles they've outgrown because leaving would feel like loss of status. Others overextend—financially or energetically—to preserve an image. Some eschew risk entirely, fearing that failure would not only affect their finances but reveal some deeper inadequacy. The underlying logic is consistent: if income equates to identity, fluctuations in earnings must reflect fluctuations in worth. The peril lies not in the importance of income, but in tying it to selfhood, which narrows freedom of movement and enforces reactivity over internal clarity.

Against this backdrop emerges the concept of the résumé economy—a cultural architecture in which professional credibility is tied to linear, institutional markers: job titles, company prestige, academic credentials, and uninterrupted timelines. This model was workable when careers were stable, employers predictable, and mobility largely linear. That world no longer exists. The modern economy—accelerated by digitalisation and decentralisation—demands fluidity and adaptive value creation. Freelancers, solopreneurs, creators, and contractors now form a significant portion of the workforce. Their contributions are real and rising, yet many feel marginalised by systems blind to non-traditional paths.

The mismatch between contribution and recognition produces a quiet legitimacy crisis. A freelance designer earning £60,000 from retained clients may have stable, high-quality work yet feel inferior to a salaried peer at a well-known brand. A hospitality worker, skilled in leadership and logistics, may internalise a "low-skilled" identity despite exceptional competence. These examples illustrate narrative distortion: when income dominates self-evaluation, the richness of achievement and growth is obscured.

A central task, then, is to name and dismantle these distortions. Income may reflect market value, but it does not capture your full worth as a human agent—or what you could earn once aligned with the right opportunities, skills, and structures. Recognition of this potential is impossible while internal ceilings remain tied to current pay.

Low income is frequently misattributed to low value, when it often signals misalignment—between skill and market, effort and leverage, time invested and outcomes realised. Many highly capable individuals remain underpaid due to structural limitations, particularly in service, care, education, and the arts. Yet internalised shame treats systemic constraints as personal failings. Escaping these low-wage traps begins with acknowledging them as structural, not individual. From there, strategies such as skill stacking, opportunity audits, and shifting from time-based to value-based pricing open new avenues—but none of this is feasible until the narrative itself is reframed.

Reframing requires permission, often more psychological than financial. Hesitation arises from the belief that pivoting signals failure or wasted years. Yet meaningful career shifts are seldom reinventions from zero; they reposition accumulated experience. A teacher becomes a learning designer, a barista a hospitality consultant, a copywriter a brand strategist. These transformations are increasingly common in a landscape that prizes adaptability and insight over narrow expertise.

What holds people back is not a scarcity of options but an internal script that insists: "I've already chosen" or "It's too late to become someone else." That script only holds power if past choices are seen as determinative of potential. They are not. Potential is defined by the capacity to learn, reposition, and act deliberately. Change begins with a sober assessment of existing assets—skills, interests, networks, underutilised knowledge. Small, deliberate shifts—new platforms, adjusted pricing models, reframed positioning—can yield disproportionate returns. Across industries, when income is decoupled from identity, strategic freedom expands.

This chapter offers frameworks to initiate that freedom. Not prescriptive formulas, but diagnostic tools: separating self-worth from payslip, deconstructing the résumé economy, engaging with a decentralised valuation landscape, recognising low-wage patterns in thought and sector, and identifying exit ramps. Most crucially, it confronts the internal permission structures that must shift for any change to endure. At its core, reclaiming financial direction is reclaiming authorship over your professional narrative.

Income is a signal, not your soul. It can—and often must—change without compromising identity. Once separated from selfhood, what remains is powerful: a person acting from clarity rather than compensation, pursuing paths guided by vision rather than vanity, seeing money as fuel rather than validation. That shift is foundational. It is the work we begin here.

Separating What You Earn from Who You Are

The conflation of income and identity is one of the most corrosive yet socially accepted distortions in modern life. From the moment young adults enter the workforce, they are met with an unspoken assumption: *your worth is measured by what you earn, and your place in society is indexed to your payslip.* It is not merely a cultural expectation—it becomes an internal compass. Titles become shorthand for value. Salaries become social proof. And before long, the distinction between what you *do* and who you *are* becomes dangerously blurred.

This conflation is rarely questioned in early adulthood, partly because it is so deeply normalised. Education systems reward students for achievements tied to future employability. Career fairs and alumni networks nudge graduates towards high-paying industries as though their economic output were the final verdict on their potential. Even casual conversations reinforce the link: "What do you do?" is universally understood as a question not just about work, but about identity. When the answer is impressive, it elevates the speaker. When it's less prestigious, it's often offered with disclaimers or apologies. The underlying logic is clear—even if unspoken: *Your income reflects your intelligence, discipline, and societal value.*

But this framework collapses under scrutiny. Consider two people: one, a venture capital analyst earning £140,000 per year; the other, a community health worker earning £32,000. One operates in an environment of speculative capital, the other in direct service to human need. One extracts value, the other delivers it. Yet in public discourse, and often in private perception, the former is seen as more successful, more evolved, even more admirable. This is not an economic observation—it's a psychological one. We have allowed earnings to replace ethics, meaning, or contribution as a dominant measure of personal worth. And the result is a generation of talented, thoughtful people who silently question their legitimacy because their payslip does not match the prestige scripts they've absorbed.

This issue is not theoretical. It has daily, measurable effects. People avoid career moves that could lead to greater alignment or purpose because those paths may reduce their earnings in the short term. Others stay in high-income roles that exhaust them, simply because the title offers them validation. Many hesitate to leave toxic work environments because they fear not only the financial instability but the loss of *identity* that comes with no longer being able to answer, "I work at [impressive company]." In each case, decisions are being governed not by strategic thinking or authentic values, but by a fear of social demotion.

The irony, of course, is that most people intellectually *know* that income is not a proxy for moral worth, insight, or personal potential. They can recognise that artists, teachers, caregivers, and entrepreneurs often contribute more value than they are paid for. But *knowing* and *internalising* are not the same. The internalisation of worth-as-wealth is a deeper psychological architecture. It is the reason someone can feel embarrassed to earn less than their friends, even if their life is otherwise deeply aligned. It is the reason a person can feel shame after being laid off—even when the event was economic, not personal. And it is the reason that financial decision-making so often becomes entangled with self-esteem.

Psychologically, this phenomenon is connected to what researchers call *contingent self-worth*—a fragile form of self-regard that depends on external outcomes. In this case, income becomes the variable upon which self-worth is pegged. When it rises, confidence rises; when it drops, self-regard plummets. This volatility is emotionally exhausting, and it creates a distorted feedback loop. Instead of asking, *Is my work meaningful? Am I growing? Do I feel in control?*, people ask, *Am I making enough to justify my choices?* And because "enough" is a moving target—always relative, always recalibrated against peers—the answer is often no.

To break this loop, the first task is conceptual clarity. *Income is a data point. It is not a diagnosis.* It tells you something about your market position, your current leverage, and perhaps your industry norms—but it tells you *nothing* definitive about your intelligence, integrity, or future trajectory. Like any data point, income becomes more useful when it is contextualised. A £40,000 salary in a low-cost region with high autonomy and flexible hours may provide more real value than £90,000 in a high-cost, high-burnout corporate job. Similarly, an inconsistent income from a growing freelance career may be more strategic in the long run than a stagnant salary with no upward path. But to see these trade-offs clearly, you have to decouple income from ego.

This decoupling is not an act of detachment—it is an act of precision. When you separate what you earn from who you are, you gain the ability to analyse your financial life without defensive emotion. You can audit your skills, value, and growth areas without interpreting every gap as a personal failing. You can experiment with new income models—consulting, digital products, royalties—without the fear that a slow start signals inadequacy. Most importantly, you can evaluate job offers, career moves, and financial goals through a lens of *alignment*, not just advancement.

It is here that alternative metrics become essential. If you are not going to use income as your identity anchor, what will you use instead? This is not a rhetorical question. Your answer matters. Some may choose metrics like autonomy, impact, creativity, or time sovereignty. Others may focus on emotional resilience, learning curve, or contribution to a particular community. These are not vague ideals—they can be tracked, measured, and optimised. But they require you to build a value system that is internally coherent, rather than externally dictated. Without that internal clarity, you will always default back to the numbers—because they are the loudest and most socially reinforced signals.

Realignment also opens up space for financial self-awareness. You can begin to distinguish between income as *fuel* and income as *identity*. Income as fuel is about enabling life design: paying for essentials, funding ambitions, supporting causes, buying time. Income as identity is about performance: looking successful, feeling superior, proving worth. The former leads to flexibility and calm. The latter leads to insecurity and performance anxiety. The difference is not in the amount—it is in the intention behind how you earn, spend, and evaluate.

It's worth examining how these dynamics play out across life stages. In your twenties, when income is often low and volatility high, the pressure to "prove yourself" through earnings can be intense. Social comparison is ubiquitous. Yet this is precisely when bold experimentation—career pivots, side hustles, alternative education—can have the highest ROI. If you defer these moves out of fear of appearing underpaid, you may preserve status at the cost of long-term compounding. Later, in your thirties or forties, when income may rise but obligations also increase, the challenge shifts. You may find yourself "golden handcuffed"—earning more than ever but less free than you were when you had less to lose. In both cases, clarity around *who you are outside of what you earn* is the hinge that enables intelligent financial design.

Real-world examples further illustrate the point. A woman leaves a high-paying job in law to start a coaching practice. Her income drops by 40% in year one, yet her quality of life improves dramatically. She tracks success not by revenue alone, but by calendar control, client satisfaction, and mental bandwidth. A university graduate turns down a corporate offer to build a small but profitable online education business. Friends are sceptical—until year three, when the business surpasses their collective salaries and offers full creative control. In both stories, income is important—but it is understood as a *means*, not a definition.

This reframing does not mean that money doesn't matter. It matters immensely. It is the lever through which you gain options, reduce stress, and invest in yourself and others. But it is *not you*. Treating income as a tool, not a testament, frees you to be more strategic, more creative, and more courageous. It makes room for risk where risk is warranted. It allows you to accept seasons of lower income—education, transition, recovery—without interpreting them as regressions. And it gives you permission to grow in non-linear ways, because growth is no longer tethered to a single number.

Separating what you earn from who you are is not a one-time revelation. It is a practice—repeated each time your self-worth is challenged by a comparison, each time you face financial uncertainty, each time you consider a move that makes emotional sense but doesn't immediately raise your income. It is a recalibration that must be done with care, consistency, and intellectual honesty. But once the separation becomes stable, your financial decisions stop feeling like identity tests. They start feeling like strategic experiments—refinements, not verdicts. And in that space, you gain not only financial clarity, but personal sovereignty.

Escaping the Résumé Economy

The conventional career path—the kind that moves neatly from education to employment to retirement—is no longer the default it once was. Yet the architecture of our economic imagination remains rooted in a paradigm where a single document, the résumé, serves as both map and merit badge. It tells employers where you've been, what you've done, and, implicitly, what you're worth. But the résumé economy, once a useful signal in a world of standardised careers, has become a limiting framework in a labour market defined by fluidity, decentralisation, and creative autonomy. It rewards legibility over potential, compliance over leverage, and linearity over innovation. And for many, escaping it is not just strategic—it's essential.

The résumé economy is built on industrial-era assumptions: that productivity is tied to hours, that career paths are best navigated through hierarchy, and that the most valuable workers are those with institutional pedigree. It privileges continuity over experimentation, institutional recognition over independent outcomes, and credentials over competence. But these assumptions no longer map onto reality. A marketing executive with ten years of experience at a household brand may struggle to adapt in a freelance or startup context where speed, experimentation, and creative risk are valued over corporate polish. Meanwhile, a 26-year-old content strategist with no formal training but a proven track record of building a 200,000-subscriber audience can monetise that influence directly—through brand partnerships, paid communities, licensing, or teaching—without ever needing to submit a CV.

This shift is not speculative. It is already playing out across the earnings landscape. Platforms like Upwork, Fiverr, and LinkedIn ProFinder have normalised project-based work. Digital storefronts like Gumroad and Etsy allow individuals to sell products, tools, and intellectual property without gatekeepers. Subscription models on Patreon or Substack give creators recurring revenue and audience intimacy. YouTube, Shopify, and TikTok have become full-stack business engines for those who understand how to pair content with commerce. None of these models rely on traditional hiring pipelines. They rely on *proof of value*, not permission.

Yet despite these evolutions, many people continue to build their economic lives as if the résumé remains their primary currency. They invest heavily in linear experience, accumulating job titles instead of transferrable skills. They hesitate to pursue entrepreneurial experiments because such ventures can't be neatly explained to future employers. They downgrade or omit freelance projects, side hustles, or passion work from their profiles, fearing they'll appear unfocused or unserious. The résumé economy has trained them to fear incoherence more than stagnation.

The irony is that the most in-demand workers today are not those with perfect résumés—they are those with *compound leverage*. That is, individuals who possess a unique combination of skills, access to audiences, ownership of assets, and control over their time. These are not qualities that appear on a CV. They are cultivated through deliberate experiments, non-linear learning, and risk-tolerant decision-making. They are built outside traditional institutions, often in public, and they rarely conform to HR templates.

Case studies illustrate this shift with striking clarity. Take Anna, a former public relations manager who left agency life after a decade to build a one-woman consultancy. She began by offering press release writing and media outreach on a freelance basis, but quickly recognised her clients needed strategic storytelling, not just execution. Over time, she layered on ghostwriting, speaker coaching, and media training—products of her existing skill set, but repackaged for higher leverage. Within three years, she was earning more than she had in her previous salaried role, with fewer hours, full creative control, and a growing portfolio of equity-based engagements. None of this was visible on a résumé. All of it was built by escaping its logic.

Or consider Daniel, a self-taught software developer who never completed a university degree. Rather than pursue traditional employment, he began contributing to open-source projects, documenting his learning in public, and building small applications he distributed via GitHub. His work caught the attention of a VC-backed startup founder, who hired him not based on his credentials, but his *visible output*. Within a year, Daniel was leading a team. Not because he followed a predictable trajectory, but because he demonstrated rare leverage: shipping ability, adaptability, and public proof of skill.

These examples are not exceptions. They are signals. The résumé economy privileges *predictability.* The emerging economy rewards *dynamism.* This is not to say that employment is obsolete. For many, a stable role within an organisation provides learning, resources, and the focus needed to master a domain. But what's changing is the understanding of *what employment is for.* Increasingly, it is a *platform*, not a destination. It is a phase in a larger sequence—one that might include side projects, entrepreneurial experiments, asset building, and independent work. And treating employment as a launchpad, not a lodestar, changes how you approach it entirely.

To escape the résumé economy is not to abandon structure or professionalism. It is to *redefine your value outside institutional formatting.* It begins with asking sharper questions. What do I know how to do that people will pay for directly? Where am I earning money in ways that don't require me to be hired? What assets—intellectual, creative, relational—am I building that could earn while I sleep or scale with minimal friction? These are not traditional career planning questions. But they are the questions that define financial sovereignty in a landscape shaped by volatility and technological acceleration.

The emotional challenge is significant. Many who grew up with conventional success scripts find it unnerving to operate outside formal structures. There's a comfort in clear benchmarks, annual reviews, and the external validation of promotions or credentials. Leaving that world—even partially—can feel like stepping off a map. But the upside is enormous. When your income is no longer gated by résumé logic, your earning potential becomes uncapped. You are no longer dependent on being chosen. You get to choose. You become, in effect, your own employer—even if you still work for others.

This shift also has profound implications for self-perception. When you stop seeing your job title as your identity, you start building identity around *capability.* You learn to define yourself by what you can *create, solve, or deliver*—not by what an employer has validated.

That's a deeper form of confidence, because it's rooted in reality, not recognition. And it holds even when roles change, industries shift, or job markets tighten.

Of course, not everyone will want to go fully independent, nor should they. The point is not to glorify freelancing or entrepreneurship as universally superior. The point is to understand that *income no longer needs to be routed through institutional channels to be legitimate, scalable, or secure.* Once that realisation is internalised, your posture changes. You stop optimising for résumé lines and start optimising for *leverage, ownership, and fit.* You become strategic in how you stack skills, how you design your work life, and how you position yourself in a fluid market.

The résumé economy trained you to wait for opportunities. Escaping it trains you to *create* them. That distinction, once understood, is irreversible. It's not about rebellion—it's about realism. The world of work has changed. Now, it's time your strategies caught up.

Low-Wage Traps and How to Exit Them

There is a category of work that is both essential and structurally underpaid. It includes the café barista with encyclopaedic product knowledge, the freelance graphic designer juggling five clients, the delivery driver coordinating logistics more efficiently than a dispatch system, the care worker operating with emotional intelligence that no algorithm can replicate. These roles demand skill, resilience, and creativity. Yet despite their value, they are frequently locked into wage ceilings that are difficult to break. This phenomenon is not merely an economic issue—it is a structural trap. And like all traps, it is maintained not just by external conditions, but by internalised limitations that make it hard to see a way out.

Low-wage traps are sustained by a combination of market dynamics, cultural narratives, and professional silos. In sectors like hospitality, education, creative services, and the gig economy, wages often stagnate regardless of skill improvement. Workers become more efficient, more reliable, more experienced—but their pay remains tethered to arbitrary rates, fixed contracts, or platform algorithms. The result is a subtle form of economic inertia: progress is made, but it doesn't compound. Days are filled, but futures remain fragile. Many in these sectors have reached a form of invisible ceiling—not because they lack ambition or competence, but because the systems around them are not designed to reward iteration.

The most dangerous aspect of a low-wage trap is that it disguises itself as stability. You are working, earning, covering bills. On the surface, you're doing what responsible adults do. But beneath that surface, the financial margin is razor-thin, and the ability to shift your trajectory is shrinking with each year spent repeating the same cycle. Over time, the repetition becomes normalised. You start to believe that earning just enough to cover your costs is the default for your profession, or worse, for someone like you. That belief—more than any employer or algorithm—cements the ceiling.

One of the most insidious myths that fuels this cycle is the idea that hard work naturally leads to higher income. In low-wage sectors, effort and output are often decoupled from compensation. You can work twelve-hour shifts, pick up extra projects, or double your client load and still remain functionally underpaid. This isn't a reflection of laziness or poor money management. It's a function of leverage—or lack thereof. In traditional low-wage roles, time is sold by the hour or by the task, with little opportunity for scale. The only way to earn more is to work more. And that model breaks down as soon as life introduces constraints: caregiving, health, burnout, or simply the limits of a 24-hour day.

Escaping this trap requires a reframing of the problem. The question is not how to hustle harder or stretch further. The question is how to *change the terms of engagement.* That begins with two foundational tools: *skill-stacking* and *opportunity auditing.* These are not abstract concepts—they are practical strategies used by individuals across sectors to move from labour-based income to value-based income. The first widens your offer. The second sharpens your aim.

Skill-stacking involves combining complementary abilities in ways that elevate your market value. It does not mean becoming a master of everything; it means creating a skill profile that is rare and economically differentiated. For example, a photographer who learns basic copywriting and social media strategy is no longer just a service provider—they become a visual storyteller who can help clients drive engagement and conversions. A customer service professional who adds project management and data visualisation becomes a cross-functional operator who can lead internal process improvements. These combinations do more than expand capabilities—they create *asymmetric value.* You become harder to replace and easier to promote—or price independently.

The power of skill-stacking lies in its ability to escape narrow definitions. Many people in low-wage work are defined by a single role: *waiter, admin assistant, dog walker, illustrator.* When you are defined by your job title, you are at the mercy of how that role is perceived in the market. When you are defined by a composite of skills, you gain strategic optionality. You can move laterally, repurpose expertise, or package your value in more flexible and profitable ways.

Opportunity auditing is the counterpart to this process. It involves taking a detailed inventory of how, where, and for whom you currently produce value—and then identifying where those dynamics can be shifted for higher return. This might mean recognising that your highest-value tasks occur outside your official job description. It might mean noticing that the clients who pay you the least are the most demanding. It might mean seeing that your income ceiling is not the result of market conditions, but of a business model that assumes linear growth. Auditing is about surfacing *leverage points*—those often-overlooked spots where small changes produce disproportionate results.

Consider the case of Jay, a full-time Uber driver in Manchester who began recording short videos about local routes, rider behaviour, and platform economics. Within a year, his YouTube channel was generating ad revenue, affiliate income, and invitations to consult with startups in the mobility space. Driving was still part of his income—but it was no longer the ceiling. Or take Liana, a freelance illustrator earning £25 per hour on commissions. After a detailed audit, she realised that the same clients repeatedly asked for licensing rights. Instead of underpricing custom work, she created a digital library of vector art, sold on a subscription basis through Gumroad and Creative Market. Within eighteen months, her passive income exceeded her client income. In both cases, the exit ramp was not a dramatic leap—it was a series of targeted recalibrations.

Critically, these exits do not require a financial cushion, elite credentials, or perfect timing. They require awareness, experimentation, and a tolerance for iteration. Most important shifts begin with modest tests: raising prices for a specific offering, pitching a new service to a past client, learning a new software tool that expands your capacity. What matters is not scale at the outset—it's *momentum*. And momentum is built through agency.

Agency, however, is often constrained by emotional narratives. People in low-wage roles frequently carry shame, fatigue, or self-doubt rooted in years of being undervalued. This emotional residue clouds judgment. You hesitate to raise prices because you fear losing clients. You resist upskilling because you assume it won't matter. You defer risk because you've absorbed the idea that survival is all you can expect. But these beliefs, while emotionally valid, are often economically outdated. The landscape has shifted. Tools, platforms, and networks now exist that make self-directed income more viable than ever before. But access to these tools is irrelevant if belief hasn't caught up.

Exiting the low-wage trap, then, is not just an economic strategy—it is a psychological pivot. It requires you to stop asking for permission and start asking sharper questions: *What unique combination of skills can I offer that few others do? Where in my workflow am I delivering more value than I'm being paid for? What can I automate, license, or scale?* These are not idle queries. They are catalysts. They reframe you not as a worker trapped in a system, but as a builder with strategic levers.

It is also worth challenging the cultural myth that moving out of low-wage work means abandoning one's roots or selling out. Economic advancement does not mean erasing your past—it means extracting lessons from it. Many of the most resilient, adaptable, and client-centric entrepreneurs today began in roles considered "low status." Their emotional intelligence, endurance, and communication skills were forged in high-stress, low-resource environments. Those qualities, when paired with strategic positioning, become a powerful competitive edge.

Every income trap has an exit. But exits don't always announce themselves. They have to be designed—through better information, sharper models, and intentional recalibration. The work is real. It is not quick. But it is available. And for those willing to step outside the narrow definitions that have long constrained their economic identity, the rewards are not just financial. They are structural. They are psychological. And they are durable. Because once you stop thinking of your income as fixed and start thinking of it as *designed*, the ceiling is no longer something to fear. It is something to dismantle. Piece by piece. Intentionally. Permanently.

Permission to Pivot

Career decisions are rarely made on logic alone. More often, they hinge on emotion—on what we think we're allowed to do, what we fear others will say, and whether we believe we've "earned" the right to change. Nowhere is this more evident than in the act of pivoting. Shifting professional direction—whether subtly or dramatically—is less about skill or timing than about *permission*. Not institutional permission, but internal: the quiet, deeply personal authorisation to reimagine who you are allowed to become.

The idea of the pivot carries an implicit narrative of reinvention. It suggests leaving something behind—identity, credibility, income stability—and reaching for something not yet proven. This perceived rupture is what makes pivots so difficult, especially for high-achieving professionals. The fear is not just that the new path might fail, but that making the move at all will signal uncertainty, risk, or regression. You worry that others will question your judgement, that you'll be seen as scattered, or worse, that you'll lose the authority you've carefully built. And so you stay put—quietly misaligned, sometimes deeply disengaged—waiting for a sign that won't arrive.

What makes this tension harder is that conventional career scripts reward linearity. Promotions, raises, and recognition are built into most organisational structures as rewards for endurance and specialisation. You are expected to climb a ladder, not redesign the building. Pivoting disrupts that logic. It means stepping off a path where you are known and stepping onto terrain where you must prove yourself again, often without the benefit of legacy credentials. The threat is existential, not just economic. The unspoken question is: *Will I still be someone if I'm no longer who I've been?*

But the cost of not pivoting is rarely discussed with equal seriousness. Staying too long in the wrong role, industry, or model of work can have consequences that compound quietly. You lose momentum. You begin to distrust your own instincts. You rationalise underperformance as loyalty, and confusion as maturity. Eventually, you internalise the limits of your current context as personal limitations. What began as a mismatch becomes a misdiagnosis. And the longer this goes unaddressed, the more psychological gymnastics are required to justify staying still.

A more constructive framing is to see pivots not as escapes, but as *strategic reorientations*. You are not discarding your past—you are repositioning it. A teacher who becomes a learning designer isn't abandoning education; they're evolving its delivery. A software engineer who shifts into product strategy isn't changing disciplines; they're expanding their field of influence. Even someone who exits their entire sector—say, from finance to wellness—is rarely starting from zero. They bring transferable insights: analytical thinking, stakeholder management, resilience under pressure. These cross-domain bridges are often more valuable than expertise alone, because they signal adaptability—a trait more predictive of long-term success than any single credential.

Still, the emotional permission to pivot often feels like the hardest part. This is where psychological frameworks become vital—not as feel-good reframes, but as rigorous tools for navigating complexity. One of the most useful is *self-concept clarity*: the degree to which your understanding of who you are is stable and internally coherent. People with low self-concept clarity often struggle with change because they fear losing their identity. But those with high clarity understand that identity is not fixed—it is layered. They can differentiate between roles and essence, between what they do and who they are. This distinction makes pivots less threatening. If you know your core values, aptitudes, and operating principles, then changing the context in which you express them becomes less destabilising and more empowering.

Another powerful concept is the *adjacent possible*, a term borrowed from complexity science. It refers to the idea that meaningful change is most sustainable when it evolves from your current capabilities and networks—not when it leaps into the unfamiliar without support. The best pivots often follow this principle. They are not wild departures but deliberate expansions into adjacent domains. A journalist builds a content strategy agency. A personal trainer launches an app. A marketing manager becomes an independent copywriter. These shifts are evolutionary, not revolutionary, and they allow you to carry forward credibility while building new leverage.

To operationalise this, one must conduct what might be called a *pivot audit*. This involves mapping three elements: (1) your current sources of energy and depletion—what parts of your work light you up or drain you; (2) your core competencies—skills that are both proven and portable; and (3) your access points—relationships, tools, or communities that can ease the transition. The intersection of these elements often reveals options that were previously obscured by anxiety or habituation. The goal is not to fantasise about a dramatic reinvention, but to identify plausible, energising directions that offer alignment without unnecessary risk.

Consider the example of Tasha, a high-performing operations manager at a logistics company. Though skilled and well-compensated, she felt stifled by the narrowness of her role. After an audit, she recognised that her strengths in systems thinking and cross-functional collaboration could be applied in consultancy. Within a few months, she secured freelance contracts helping small businesses build internal processes. She didn't burn bridges—she expanded her bandwidth. Her pivot was not an identity crisis; it was a design choice.

Contrast this with Ravi, a freelance web developer who had grown increasingly disengaged from client work. His audit revealed that what energised him wasn't development per se, but teaching. Rather than abandon tech entirely, he began creating educational content—courses, livestreams, and paid workshops. Over time, this content replaced his client income and gave him greater autonomy. Both Tasha and Ravi pivoted strategically—not from burnout, but from insight.

This distinction matters. Many people attempt to pivot reactively, as an escape from toxic environments or chronic boredom. While these impulses are understandable, pivots driven by avoidance often fail to sustain momentum. The new path may bring temporary relief, but without clarity on what you're pivoting *toward*, you risk recreating the same conditions in a new form. Emotional permission, then, must be paired with strategic intention. You must be honest not only about what you're leaving, but about what you're building.

Part of granting yourself that permission is dismantling the myth of irreversibility. A pivot is not a one-way door. You are allowed to test, to pause, to recalibrate. Career decisions do not require permanence to be valid. This is particularly important in an age of portfolio work, where many people move between roles, domains, and income models multiple times. The fear of choosing "wrong" is often paralysing—but in practice, most decisions are iterative. You adjust as you go. And the skills, relationships, and insights you gain along the way are rarely wasted.

It's also worth acknowledging that pivoting can surface emotional residue—feelings of guilt, grief, or perceived failure. You may mourn the version of yourself you thought you'd become. You may feel disloyal to mentors or colleagues. You may struggle with impostor syndrome in your new context. These feelings are not weaknesses; they are part of the recalibration process. But they do require emotional regulation, community support, and self-compassion. Without those, the pivot can feel isolating and destabilising. With them, it becomes a rite of maturity.

The most effective pivots do not require you to burn out or burn bridges. They require you to ask better questions. *What is my core value, and how else could it be expressed? Where is my effort underpriced or misaligned? What adjacent moves would increase both fulfilment and earning potential?* These questions lead not to fantasy, but to *design.* And once you see your career as something you can design—not simply endure or perform—you become infinitely more resilient.

Permission to pivot is not granted by the market, your manager, or even your résumé. It's granted by your willingness to honour misalignment as information, not failure. It is the quiet, sovereign act of saying: *The version of me that made past decisions did so intelligently—but I am no longer bound by their assumptions.* That realisation is not just liberating. It's foundational. Because once you learn to pivot deliberately, you stop fearing reinvention—and start mastering it.

Chapter 3
Spend with Eyes Open

Spending is too often treated as the least thoughtful aspect of personal finance—a behaviour to be constrained, tracked, or optimised, but seldom examined for meaning. Conventional financial advice frames it mechanically: money in, money out. Budgeting apps, frugality hacks, minimalist mantras dominate, all carrying the same unspoken premise—spending is the problem, and the objective is minimisation. But what if that premise is fundamentally flawed? What if spending is not merely a reflection of discipline, but a window into identity? What if the choices we make with money reveal memory, values, self-concept—even unresolved trauma?

This chapter opens with a simple yet radical idea: every pound you spend tells a story. Not merely a transactional record, but an emotional footprint. How we spend encodes priorities, assumptions, and internalised beliefs about worth, scarcity, safety, and success. Most of these narratives operate beneath conscious awareness. When surfaced, however, they become potent levers for transformation—not solely financially, but personally.

True financial intelligence is not just the capacity to read compound interest charts or diversify an index fund—it is the ability to interpret your own behaviour. Why that purchase, in that moment, with that justification? Why certain categories consistently overrun budgets? Why does money feel secure in some contexts, threatening in others? These are not spreadsheet questions; they are questions of self-awareness. And their answers illuminate trajectories far more clearly than any budgeting tool ever could.

Money has a memory—not just because bank statements record choices, but because behavioural patterns repeat. Many financial behaviours are inherited scripts. Perhaps you grew up in a household where spending was impulsive and unexamined, associating money with fleeting highs and lingering regret. Or perhaps scarcity dominated, instilling guilt with every purchase and leaving investment in growth fraught with anxiety. Money might have been a source of conflict, secrecy, or power play, producing oscillations between control and avoidance.

Recognising these patterns is not about blame; it is about authorship. You cannot design a healthy financial life while unconsciously acting out someone else's story. What appears as a lack of discipline is often inherited behaviour. What seems like irresponsibility may be a defence mechanism, laid down in childhood, reinforced culturally, and rarely examined. Traditional budgeting advice often fails for this reason: it treats behaviour as technical rather than emotional. Until you confront the why behind your spending, any new system will eventually bend to the old logic.

Take the notion of "cheapness" as a virtue. Many pride themselves on finding deals, delaying gratification, spending as little as possible. Superficially, this seems prudent. Yet closer inspection often reveals a hidden emotional cost. Cheap choices carry trade-offs: time lost navigating complexity, quality sacrificed for short-term savings, relationships strained by inflexibility. Frugality can be exhausting, draining joy, spontaneity, and even long-term wealth.

This is the emotional cost of cheap. It manifests subtly: purchasing flimsy products that need frequent replacement, declining social invitations that foster belonging, avoiding tools or services that could multiply capability. The immediate "win" of saving masks deeper losses—of vitality, efficiency, opportunity. Over time, such a posture trains low expectations—from life, from others, and from oneself. Survival is prioritised over expansion. The spreadsheet may look healthy, but the person behind it feels diminished.

This is not an argument for indulgence, but for discernment. The goal is not simply to spend more, but to spend better—in ways that reinforce values, energise commitments, and support a future vision.

Tracking spending becomes a tool for clarity, not punishment. Patterns emerge. Purchases that nourish, distract, or anchor one to outdated identities become evident. Suddenly, the bank statement reads less like numbers and more like a self-portrait—and the edits are obvious.

A powerful technique is the spending audit. Unlike conventional audits that focus on categories or totals, this approach interrogates meaning. For each significant purchase, ask: what emotion preceded it? What belief justified it? What identity did it reinforce? You might find overspending in response to inadequacy, underinvestment in personal growth due to a belief that you must "earn" the right to flourish, or trivial purchases settling emotional debts. This is pattern recognition, not oversensitivity. Patterns can be redesigned once identified.

Central to that redesign is distinguishing sustainable joy from disposable dopamine. Sustainable joy delivers long-term satisfaction; disposable dopamine provides fleeting escape, often followed by emptiness. Modern consumer culture is optimised for the latter. Targeted ads, frictionless checkout, instant gratification—all engineer impulse over alignment. Awareness of this dynamic grants agency: you become designer rather than participant.

Neuroscience supports this distinction. Anticipated purchases that align with long-term goals activate reward systems differently than impulsive acquisitions. Self-congruent purchases—those affirming identity and purpose—produce durable satisfaction. Purchases driven by emotional discomfort often reinforce stress. This is not moralising; it is neurobiological fact. The implication is clear: pause before buying. Ask: will this reinforce who I am becoming, or temporarily soothe who I am trying to avoid?

To spend consciously is not to spend less, but to spend intentionally. Money becomes a language, not merely a control system. Each purchase is a sentence. What are you saying? Who are you becoming?

This chapter invites reclaiming authorship over that language. It guides you to identify and release inherited spending scripts, exposes the hidden costs of chronic cheapness, and introduces frameworks—grounded in neuroscience and behavioural psychology—for favouring sustainable joy over momentary stimulation.

By the end, your eyes will be sharper—not only for what you purchase, but for what your spending says about your identity. More importantly, you will see who you are capable of becoming.

Your Money Has a Memory

Most people think of money as a tool—cold, neutral, objective. It enters, it exits, it either adds up or it doesn't. But this view is insufficient. Money is not just a medium of exchange; it is a repository of meaning. Every pound spent carries with it a narrative: of how we see ourselves, what we value, what we fear, what we aspire to, and what we're compensating for. Your spending habits are not isolated economic events; they are behavioural artefacts, tracing a psychological lineage of beliefs, assumptions, and identity. In that sense, *your money has a memory*, and learning to read that memory may be the most important financial skill you never learned.

The history of a single transaction is rarely as simple as want, purchase, satisfaction. Behind every spending choice is a web of emotions—some obvious, others barely perceptible. A last-minute impulse buy may be triggered by anxiety. A luxury upgrade could stem from a need to prove worth. A refusal to spend on therapy, coaching, or upskilling may signal a belief that investing in oneself is unjustified or indulgent. These aren't just spending decisions—they're value declarations, often unconscious, shaped by past environments, cultural conditioning, and early economic experiences.

This makes spending a particularly rich site for self-inquiry. Unlike abstract financial goals or long-term investment strategies, spending happens daily. It's immediate. Tangible. And therefore, it provides a real-time mirror of who we are becoming. But most people look away. We avoid reviewing bank statements, delete app notifications, and compartmentalise "needs" and "wants" in ways that obscure the deeper question: *what story is this spending choice telling about me—and do I agree with it?*

Understanding your money's memory requires rejecting the dominant narrative that financial tracking is about restriction. When spending review is framed as punishment, we instinctively rebel. It feels infantilising, like being told off for bad behaviour. But reframed as a form of awareness, tracking becomes an act of agency. You're not being audited—you're conducting an inquiry. Not, *"Where did I go wrong?"* but, *"What was I believing in that moment—and is it still true?"* This is the key pivot. It moves the conversation from guilt to growth, from shame to clarity.

To illustrate this, consider the spending behaviour of someone raised in a financially unstable household. As an adult, they might exhibit hoarding tendencies—not just of material goods, but of opportunities to "stockpile" perceived safety. This can manifest in overconsumption of discounted items, obsessive deal-hunting, or extreme reluctance to invest in quality. On the surface, it looks like thrift. But underneath is a survival script, rooted in the belief that the future is unsafe and must be controlled through accumulation. Unless that belief is examined, no amount of budgeting will feel sufficient.

Contrast that with someone raised in an affluent but emotionally distant environment, where love or validation was offered through gifts rather than connection. They may grow up equating spending with affection—both giving and receiving. Their adult financial life may feature cycles of generous gift-giving or shopping sprees during emotional lows. Again, the issue isn't the behaviour per se—it's the *belief it expresses*, often unconsciously: "Spending is how I express love or find relief." Without awareness, this leads to financial misalignment masked as generosity or emotional self-care.

These examples reveal a crucial insight: *our financial behaviours often predate our financial decisions.* The money is simply the medium through which unresolved dynamics express themselves. This is why traditional advice about "cutting back" or "being smarter with money" so often fails. It addresses the symptom without interrogating the system that produced it.

To change this, we must approach spending with the mindset of a documentarian. Observe first. Interpret second. Resist the urge to immediately judge your habits. Instead, ask: *What patterns keep repeating? When do I feel most in control financially—and when do I tend to override that control? What situations trigger financial impulsivity, rigidity, or avoidance?* Then go deeper: *What core belief is being reinforced through this behaviour? Where did I learn that belief? Do I still agree with it?*

For example, someone may consistently under-spend on their health—delaying dental visits, avoiding gym memberships, refusing to buy decent footwear. On a spreadsheet, this might look like "practical restraint." But a deeper analysis may reveal a sense of unworthiness or a belief that others' needs come first. By tracking that habit, and surfacing the belief underneath, they are given the choice to revise it. The moment that belief becomes visible is the moment it becomes optional.

This is the true power of spending awareness—not micromanagement, but narrative revision. It allows you to see that money is not a neutral tool, but a carrier of assumptions about who you are, what matters, and what's possible. When your financial choices consistently contradict your stated values, the result is internal conflict. But when your spending becomes a form of aligned expression, it can feel as though your finances are an extension of your ethics—your wallet matches your worldview.

The practical implications of this are profound. It means that spending plans should be designed *around identity*, not just categories. Rather than setting a generic monthly budget, ask: *What kind of person am I becoming? What does that person spend money on? What do they no longer tolerate?* A creative who wants to reclaim their time might need to redirect spending from short-term dopamine (like endless streaming subscriptions) into tools that amplify output or create white space. An emerging leader might choose to invest in high-trust relationships—through travel, coaching, or quality time—instead of letting money stagnate in categories that preserve comfort but not growth.

This reframing turns spending into a values alignment exercise. When done well, it increases not only financial clarity, but psychological congruence. You begin to trust yourself more—not because you're "sticking to a budget," but because your financial behaviour now reflects your inner compass. That trust becomes the foundation for bigger, bolder decisions—quitting a job, launching a project, setting new boundaries—because you are no longer living in conflict between your spreadsheet and your soul.

It also inoculates you against a dangerous cultural trend: the over-intellectualisation of finance. In the digital age, we are inundated with optimisation tools, financial jargon, and endless tips for getting the "most" out of every pound. But this kind of hyper-optimisation can easily become a smokescreen. It gives the illusion of control while obscuring the deeper issue: *Are you building a financial life that reflects who you really are—or just one that looks efficient?* This is the uncomfortable truth behind many people's spending habits. They are "successful" on paper but feel deeply disconnected from their finances because they've been outsourcing their values to other people's systems.

To resist this, you must create your own system—one informed not just by maths, but by memory. This involves developing a practice of spending reflection. Not every day, and not obsessively. But regularly enough to maintain awareness. This might mean reviewing your last five purchases and noting what motivated them. It might mean asking, *Would I make that same choice again, from a place of alignment?* Over time, this becomes less about correction and more about coherence. You are not just trying to spend "better"—you are trying to spend *truer*.

Your money's memory is always active. The question is whether you're listening. If you are, you'll find that your finances become less chaotic, not through stricter control, but through greater congruence. Spending becomes a tool for authorship, not avoidance. And when that shift occurs, you stop asking, *"How do I make better financial choices?"* and start asking, *"What kind of life am I funding—and is it mine?"*

The Emotional Cost of "Cheap"

There is a persistent myth in modern finance that equates frugality with wisdom. The cultural script is clear: cut back, do without, resist temptation. The virtuous path, we're told, is paved with minimalism, coupon codes, and disciplined denial. But beneath this surface narrative lies a more complicated truth: sometimes, *cheap costs more.* Not just in pounds, but in stress, wasted time, and lost opportunities. While frugality can be a tool for intentional living, it can also mask deeper patterns of fear, scarcity, and self-sabotage. The challenge is learning to distinguish between resourcefulness and restriction—between values-based spending and compulsive under-investment in your own wellbeing.

The financial world is obsessed with saving tactics. Entire ecosystems exist to help you find cheaper alternatives—discount flight trackers, cashback apps, and endless lists of "money-saving hacks." But few ask the more important question: *at what cost?* There is a difference between economising and impoverishing. Choosing a lower-cost option is not inherently smart. It is only smart if it preserves or enhances your quality of life, energy, or future earning potential. If it introduces hidden burdens—like constant decision fatigue, stress, or degraded performance—then the cheap option becomes expensive in ways that don't show up on your bank statement.

Consider the working professional who refuses to pay for reliable transport and instead builds their life around multiple convoluted transfers to save a few pounds each day. On paper, the decision is rational: they're cutting commuting costs. But zoom out. What's the emotional toll of that decision? Chronic lateness. Elevated stress. Lost hours of focus or rest. Missed opportunities to think, learn, or connect. Over months and years, the psychological drag of "cheapness" becomes profound. And the worst part? It often goes unnoticed—because the decision is still framed as being financially responsible.

This is where the distinction between price and cost becomes crucial. *Price* is what you pay. *Cost* is what it takes from you. A lower price does not guarantee a lower cost. Cheap shoes that damage your posture, a flimsy chair that leads to back pain, or a laptop that slows your work by 30% each day—these are all examples of false frugality. You save in the short term and bleed silently in the long term, often without making the connection. The logic of "I got it on sale" overshadows the reality of "I'm underperforming, exhausted, or frustrated because I keep surrounding myself with low-leverage tools."

This logic becomes especially corrosive when applied to personal development. Many people balk at the idea of paying for a mentor, a course, or a coach. The common refrain is, "I'll just figure it out myself." There's an implicit pride in being self-made. But here's the paradox: those most obsessed with proving they can do it alone often pay the highest price in time. They accumulate years of trial and error that could have been compressed into weeks with the right support. The cost of "saving money" becomes missed compounding—of skills, confidence, and progress.

This phenomenon is amplified by a culture that prizes independence while quietly punishing perceived indulgence. Especially among younger professionals, there is a deep tension between financial prudence and psychological permission to spend in ways that elevate one's life. A modest upgrade—say, a better-quality desk for someone working remotely—can trigger disproportionate guilt, even if the investment would increase output, comfort, and health. That guilt is rarely about the item itself; it's about an internalised belief that comfort must be earned, or that thriving too early is irresponsible.

This emotional friction is not accidental—it is cultural. Many people, especially those from working-class or immigrant backgrounds, have been conditioned to equate deprivation with virtue. Sacrifice is morally charged. Spending on oneself, particularly in non-essential ways, is framed as selfish or wasteful. These beliefs are often inherited, not chosen. And until they are surfaced and questioned, they quietly dictate behaviour that feels "wise" but is actually rooted in fear and legacy narratives. The question is no longer, *"Is this a good deal?"* but, *"Whose voice am I obeying when I choose less for myself—even when more is available?"*

At a societal level, cheapness is often marketed as empowerment. Budget airlines don't just offer low fares—they offer a philosophy: that you are clever for outsmarting the system. Discount stores don't just save you money—they make you feel savvy, like an insider. The emotional manipulation is subtle but powerful. It appeals to both the ego and the insecurity: the desire to win, and the fear of falling behind. But again, the long-term question remains: *What are you trading away in this pursuit of "smart" spending?* Sometimes, the real loss is not financial—it's psychological erosion, the slow wearing down of your sense of worth.

The workplace offers its own illustration. A creative professional undercharges to remain "accessible" and not seem greedy. A consultant offers discounts before being asked, fearing they'll be rejected otherwise. A freelancer accepts a demanding client for minimal pay, rationalising it as "better than nothing." These choices are rarely about money alone. They're about perceived value—and how it's been internalised. When you chronically under-earn or under-price, you are not just losing income—you are reinforcing a script that says your time and talent are negotiable. And that belief, once embedded, becomes self-fulfilling.

That's why the antidote to toxic cheapness is not reckless spending. It's *aligned investment.* The point is not to abandon budgeting, but to upgrade your decision-making criteria. Ask not just, *"Can I afford this?"* but, *"What does this choice signal about my priorities?"* Spending decisions should be run through multiple filters—financial, yes, but also energetic, emotional, and strategic. Does this purchase reduce future friction? Does it restore time or focus? Does it amplify my output, elevate my environment, or deepen my capacity for meaningful work?

This is particularly relevant when we examine purchases that impact your future earning potential. A better laptop for a writer. A project management tool for a solopreneur. A therapist or coach for someone navigating burnout. These are not luxuries; they are infrastructure. Just as businesses invest in high-functioning teams, systems, and assets, individuals must learn to do the same. Otherwise, you are building your life on unstable scaffolding, then wondering why you keep collapsing under pressure.

The path forward requires a new form of literacy: emotional cost accounting. It means learning to track not just your outflows in pounds and pence, but in energy, attention, and opportunity. It means recognising that decisions made in the name of frugality can sometimes be a form of slow self-erasure. And it means owning the truth that *cheap isn't always smart, and expensive isn't always foolish.* The real measure of a financial decision is not the price tag, but the life it builds—or erodes.

To cultivate this literacy, start by identifying where cheapness has cost you in the past. Was it a low-cost hire that led to high-maintenance fallout? A bargain gadget that kept malfunctioning? A string of "free" webinars that ate up your evenings with no return? Once you surface those patterns, don't just correct them—interrogate them. What belief drove that decision? And what new standard do you need to set to prevent it repeating?

This isn't about perfection. It's about discernment. The goal is not to spend more indiscriminately, but to spend *more wisely and courageously*. To say yes to things that sustain you, even if they challenge your internalised scarcity scripts. And to say no to things that drain you, even if they come disguised as deals. This requires a redefinition of what it means to be "good with money." Not someone who hoards or hesitates, but someone who chooses boldly, aligned with values, and conscious of the full cost—seen and unseen.

The future of personal finance belongs not to the most frugal, but to the most *aligned*. The ones who know that cheapness can be a disguise for fear, and that real wealth is measured not just in net worth, but in how intelligently, ethically, and joyfully we allocate our finite resources. When you stop being seduced by "cheap," you start making decisions from self-trust rather than self-doubt. And that shift changes everything.

How to Audit Your Spending Story

Money may be counted in currency, but it is written in narrative. Every pound you spend is an expression—of what you value, what you fear, what you believe about time, status, safety, and self-worth. Yet most budgeting advice treats spending as a technical behaviour, not a psychological act. It assumes that if you know where your money goes, you will change how it flows. But awareness without interpretation is insufficient. The real work lies not in tracking the *what*, but in understanding the *why*. This is the essence of a spending audit—not just tallying expenses, but decoding them. Done well, it's less an exercise in frugality and more an inquiry into identity.

Consider this: when you scroll through a bank statement, you're not simply reviewing transactions—you're reviewing habits, priorities, beliefs. That £90 spent on ride-shares last month may not be about laziness or convenience; it might reflect a refusal to waste time, an unspoken need for control, or anxiety about unpredictable public transport. A recurring takeaway bill may not signal indulgence but the exhaustion of someone working unsustainable hours. In this sense, *your spending is not random—it is rational, given your internal logic at the time of purchase.* But that logic is rarely interrogated. And so it persists, unquestioned and unchanged.

Traditional budgeting methods often fail precisely because they bypass this layer. They offer prescriptions—spend less here, cut back there—without pausing to ask: *What stories are these habits reinforcing? What unmet needs are they trying to satisfy? What version of the future are they quietly funding—or undermining?* Without these questions, budgets become brittle systems of restraint. And brittle systems break under pressure.

A proper spending audit begins not with numbers, but with context. You are not just a consumer; you are a narrator. And the plot you are writing is either aligned with your values or veering away from them. That alignment cannot be measured in spreadsheets alone. It shows up in how you feel after a purchase: energised or regretful, expansive or dulled. It reveals itself in whether you're buying things to enhance life—or to escape from it. And it becomes most visible when you begin to ask yourself—not as critic, but as curious witness—*What was I hoping this would solve?*

Let's take the example of someone who consistently spends on fitness classes they rarely attend. At first glance, the behaviour appears wasteful. But peel back the layers, and it may reveal something more meaningful—a desire to reclaim agency over health, a longing for structure, or a deep-seated belief that paying for something might unlock the discipline they feel they lack. Seen through this lens, the "bad spending" is not a flaw; it's a signal. The audit, then, is not about shaming the choice—but investigating what truth it points to.

This approach transforms the process from punitive to revelatory. You are not just cutting costs; you are discovering self-contradictions. You may realise, for instance, that you say you value financial independence, but regularly outsource minor problems for convenience. Or that you prioritise creativity and flexibility, but your spending centres around rigid status markers—branded clothes, high-end subscriptions, dinners meant to impress. These aren't moral failings; they're artefacts of a life that may have drifted from its intended design.

And that's the real power of a spending audit: it reveals whether your money is working *for* your values—or merely echoing your past. Many people are shocked to find how much of their financial behaviour is shaped by inherited scripts. A child of frugal parents might overspend to rebel. A first-generation professional might hoard money out of fear of sliding backwards. A burned-out employee might spend compulsively on gadgets as a proxy for progress. In each case, the numbers don't just reflect spending habits; they reflect psychological patterns. Without an audit, these patterns remain invisible. With one, they become optional.

To perform a meaningful audit, start by categorising your spending not by type—rent, groceries, utilities—but by intention. Try tagging each transaction with a primary driver: *security, escape, aspiration, connection, efficiency, identity, or avoidance.* This method surfaces the emotional currents running beneath your purchases. You may find that your highest recurring expenses are about maintaining appearances, not fulfilling needs. Or that you are habitually under-investing in areas that matter deeply—like health, education, or creativity—while over-spending on short-term anaesthetics.

Equally important is recognising the temporal orientation of your spending. Are you funding your *past, present,* or *future*? Many people unconsciously funnel income into compensating for past experiences—paying off debts, covering family obligations, or repairing childhood deprivation. Others over-prioritise the present—spending heavily on comfort, experience, or status while postponing investments in skills, resilience, or autonomy. A rare few tilt their resources heavily toward the future, sometimes to the detriment of present wellbeing. None of these is inherently right or wrong, but imbalance creates tension. The audit helps restore proportion.

A second lens is value-per-pound. Not in economic terms, but in *personal resonance*. Which purchases yielded the most return in joy, clarity, momentum, or support? Which left you feeling hollow, regretful, or conflicted? Create a subjective "return on investment" column beside your transactions—not just for judgement, but for learning. You might find that the £200 spent on a solo writing retreat yielded more renewal than a month's worth of impulse shopping. Or that the £12 coffee with a mentor moved your thinking further than a £500 online course. These insights are not captured in conventional budgets—but they are vital for designing a life aligned with your definition of wealth.

The final step is to narrate forward. Once you've surfaced your patterns and assigned emotional logic to your spending, ask: *What story do I want my money to tell next?* Who do I need to become for that story to be true? And what financial behaviours would that version of me embody? This shift from retrospective analysis to intentional authorship is the difference between maintenance and evolution. Budgeting becomes less about restriction, and more about *direction*. You are not just preventing waste—you are allocating energy toward a vision.

This is where the deeper transformation occurs. Because ultimately, a spending audit is not about numbers—it is about alignment. You begin to see that every pound is a vote. Not just for a product or service, but for a worldview, a habit, a self-concept. And once you realise you are voting constantly, your choices change. You stop defaulting to convenience. You pause before trying to "treat yourself" in ways that deplete you. You begin to spend not just with awareness, but with *intention*—selecting not only what meets your needs, but what reinforces your evolving identity.

Done well, this process can have profound ripple effects. You become more resistant to external scripts—advertising, social comparison, peer pressure. You build resilience against impulse. You develop a more intimate relationship with your financial ecosystem—not as a battlefield, but as a canvas. And over time, you find yourself less reactive, more centred, and more sovereign. Because the story you are telling with your money is no longer inherited or unconscious. It is authored.

And that may be the most radical financial move of all.

Sustainable Joy vs. Disposable Dopamine-

A curious paradox lies at the heart of modern spending: the more choices we have, the less satisfaction we seem to derive from them. The digital age has enabled the near-instant fulfilment of desires that, just a generation ago, would have required weeks of planning or patience. Yet the very convenience of consumption has dulled its reward. The issue isn't that people spend too much—it's that they often spend reflexively, on things that stimulate the brain's reward circuitry without actually nourishing the self. Neuroscience has begun to unravel why: many of our purchases activate dopamine pathways linked to *anticipation*, not fulfilment. The consequence is a pattern of compulsive consumption chasing novelty, while leaving meaning behind.

At the core of this lies a misunderstanding of pleasure itself. Dopamine, the neurotransmitter most often associated with reward, is not a signal of satisfaction—it is a signal of *wanting*. It spikes not when we receive the thing, but when we *expect* to receive it. This is why the scroll through an online catalogue or the arrival of a delivery notification often feels more thrilling than the object itself. The modern economy—particularly its digital interfaces—has become astonishingly adept at hijacking this loop. Apps, ads, and algorithms are designed to trigger anticipatory dopamine bursts, promising small hits of novelty in exchange for small (but frequent) expenses. The result? A culture of disposable dopamine: transactions that satisfy momentary impulses but leave little emotional residue.

Contrast this with sustainable joy—experiences or investments that may not deliver a sharp hit of excitement, but yield prolonged emotional resonance. Think of a well-spent afternoon with close friends, a solo hike that clears your mind, or a long-postponed course that reignites your intellectual curiosity. These moments rarely offer the immediate rush of, say, a flash sale purchase—but they generate *serotonin-rich* states linked to contentment, connection, and self-authorship. They are slower to form, less marketable, and harder to gamify—but infinitely more durable. Neuroscience literature increasingly supports this dichotomy: while dopamine drives goal-seeking behaviour, serotonin and oxytocin underpin the enduring states of wellbeing most people ultimately crave.

Financially speaking, the cost of chasing disposable dopamine is rarely measured in the price tag alone. It comes in the form of mental clutter—drawers full of gadgets we no longer use, wardrobes stuffed with clothes that never quite fit, subscriptions that bleed our accounts unnoticed. It accrues in decision fatigue and creeping self-doubt, as we mistake activity for agency and novelty for meaning. Over time, this pattern chips away at our sense of control, not because we've spent extravagantly, but because we've spent inattentively.

It's easy to assume that this kind of spending is harmless because it occurs in small increments. A £7 takeaway coffee here, a £12 app there. But behavioural economists have shown that the cumulative effect of these low-friction purchases can be disproportionately large—not only financially, but psychologically. They normalise impulse over intention, weakening the neural pathways associated with delay of gratification. In a world where financial literacy often focuses on numbers and spreadsheets, the more subtle skill is emotional regulation. Those who master it aren't just better at saving; they're better at discerning what is truly worth buying—because they've clarified what is worth *feeling*.

Designing a financial life oriented around sustainable joy requires a shift from reaction to reflection. One approach is to build *pacing mechanisms* into your purchasing decisions. This could be as simple as the "48-hour rule" for non-essential items or as structured as a personal filter: *Does this align with my long-term values? Will it still matter to me in six months? Is this a treat, a tool, or a trap?* These questions don't just delay the dopamine rush—they interrupt the automaticity of consumption, forcing engagement with the deeper motivations beneath it.

Equally critical is to reframe what "value" means. Our economic culture tends to conflate value with price and visibility: the more expensive or outwardly impressive a thing is, the more valuable it must be. But genuine value is subjective, often invisible, and almost always contextual. A £25 journaling retreat might shift your mindset more profoundly than a £1,000 holiday package designed to distract you from your dissatisfaction. Sustainable joy often arises from investments that may appear modest in scale but are profound in impact. They offer depth over dazzle, reflection over escape.

This lens also calls for a more generous interpretation of frugality. True frugality is not about deprivation—it is about discernment. It's not about saying no to pleasure, but about saying yes only to pleasure that sustains. Cheap dopamine tricks you into thinking you're living fully, when in fact you're avoiding the harder, more meaningful work of crafting a coherent life. A life of sustainable joy costs more in thought, not necessarily in money. It requires understanding what truly energises you, even if that means saying no to things everyone else seems to be saying yes to.

There is also a social dimension to this reorientation. Much of disposable spending is performative. We buy things not to enjoy them in private, but to signal taste, success, or inclusion. The emotional cost here is subtle but real: we become curators of image rather than stewards of experience. Sustainable joy, by contrast, often lacks an audience. It arises in private rituals, long conversations, or investments in skills and self-expression that may never be applauded. But it is in these moments that the quiet architecture of a fulfilled life is built.

To be clear, the point is not to moralise spending. There is nothing inherently wrong with enjoying convenience, entertainment, or even indulgence. The danger lies in confusing transient stimulation for actual nourishment. Neuroscientists distinguish between *hedonic* (pleasure-seeking) and *eudaimonic* (meaning-oriented) forms of wellbeing. The former can be fleeting and addictive. The latter is deeper, slower, and often requires discomfort upfront—like the discipline to practise an instrument, the vulnerability of therapy, or the risk of creative work. Financial decisions made in service of eudaimonic wellbeing may not generate dopamine spikes—but they do generate direction, resilience, and identity.

Ultimately, the question is not whether to spend, but *what your spending is reinforcing*. Is it amplifying your awareness, or distracting you from it? Is it cultivating your capacity for presence, or feeding your need for escape? Is it strengthening your ability to wait for what matters, or diluting your attention across endless options that don't?

Sustainable joy cannot be bought—but it can be funded. It lives in aligned purchases, thoughtful generosity, investment in capacity, and the courage to abstain when others indulge. It lives in the quiet spaces between transactions, where clarity takes root. And it offers something dopamine never can: the stability of knowing that your money, your time, and your attention are working not just for pleasure, but for purpose.

Chapter 4
Break the Debt Spell

Debt is rarely just a matter of arithmetic; it carries with it a weight that is cultural, emotional, and deeply personal. For millions navigating an economy marked by instability, debt seeps beyond the balance sheet. It shapes identity, rewrites futures, and bends decisions. It tells a story—often one that starts long before a first loan is signed and rarely concerns money alone.

To grasp debt fully, one must look past numbers. Traditional advice treats it mechanically: interest rates, minimum payments, amortisation schedules. These are important, yet they miss the deeper driver of chronic indebtedness—beliefs. Beliefs that taking on debt proves worth, that survival depends on credit, that escape is impossible. These internalised scripts, forged by upbringing, marketing, and institutional design, bind as tightly as any promissory note. Without examining—and rewriting—them, even the most carefully constructed repayment plan is likely to falter.

Shame often eclipses the debt itself. It is one of the few socially sanctioned forms of suffering that must be endured quietly. Unlike illness or professional setbacks, debt is framed as personal failure rather than structural circumstance. Worse, shame is self-reinforcing: it discourages review of statements, delays seeking help, and prompts minimum payments—not laziness, but avoidance hijacking the mind. Chronic shame shifts cognitive focus from action to evasion, prioritising short-term relief over long-term repair.

Modern debt frequently arises from necessity rather than frivolity. Student loans, once heralded as "investments in the future," now offer uneven returns. Medical debt is often the price of staying alive. Credit card debt can be a lifeline for those whose earnings are irregular or insufficient. Yet, once incurred, narratives change. Borrowers are labelled "irresponsible" or "bad with money," language that isolates rather than empowers.

This chapter reframes the conversation: debt is a system, not a sentence. Systems can be analysed, navigated, and altered. A person in debt is not broken, but operating in a structure without adequate support or options. Here, the focus goes beyond spreadsheets. The aim is to disentangle self-worth from balance sheets, to understand emotional patterns sustaining indebtedness, and to reclaim agency from financial paralysis.

A liberating shift is to view debt as a dynamic narrative rather than a static object. Stories have arcs, turning points, and resolutions. The goal is not to deny the hardship of debt, but to move from passive experience to authored engagement. Repayment becomes more than financial housekeeping—it becomes an exercise in emotional intelligence, planning capacity, and resilience. Seen this way, clearing debt is a foundational act of self-leadership.

Several repayment frameworks exist—not as universal solutions, but as adaptable structures. The avalanche method appeals to those driven by efficiency; the snowball method offers early psychological wins; hybrids allow for contextual customisation. Success depends not on objective superiority, but on alignment with one's psychology, stress profile, and cognitive bandwidth. Plans that disregard emotional realities fail not from flawed arithmetic, but from unsustainable process.

Equally critical is preparing for life after debt. Many assume that debt-free status guarantees confidence, yet without deliberate planning, habits that created debt may reassert themselves. The chapter addresses forward-looking credit strategies: using credit as a tool rather than a crutch, rebuilding scores in service of meaningful objectives, and engaging debt discerningly. Healthy credit functions as leverage—for mobility, business, or housing—not as lifestyle subsidy.

Beyond tactics, the chapter dismantles debt mythology: that a FICO score defines character, that financial missteps signal moral failure, that debt indicates laziness rather than systemic forces. These myths persist precisely because shame and silence reinforce them. Naming them, examining them with clarity and compassion, is the first step to disarmament.

Debt is also multigenerational—transmitted not only via balances, but via beliefs. Children witnessing financial stress or secrecy are statistically more likely to recreate it. Yet when one individual interrupts the cycle—not just by repayment, but by reframing debt—they create a new pattern, a signal in the noise. This is literacy at its most intimate, most revolutionary.

Debt is not a character flaw. It does not measure intelligence, potential, or worth. It is a predictable intersection of structural design and human vulnerability. No matter how long it has weighed upon you, the story is still being written—and you hold far more authorship than you may have realised.

Breaking the debt spell is more than adjusting balances; it is changing assumptions—about yourself, about possibility, and about the purpose of money. It is moving from apology to strategy, from hiding to planning, from coping to leading. Ultimately, it is reclaiming the mental space debt occupies and transforming it into clarity, purpose, and meaningful growth.

Debt as a Story, Not Just a Statement-

Debt is often framed as a simple arithmetic outcome: the accumulation of borrowed sums plus interest, due to be repaid over time. But this framing, while technically accurate, is dangerously incomplete. Debt is not only a financial arrangement—it is a narrative architecture. It reflects a set of beliefs, emotions, habits, and historical patterns. Debt doesn't just tell you what someone owes. It tells you what they fear, how they were raised, what they believe is possible, and where they may feel powerless. For many, especially younger adults, debt becomes less about what they borrowed and more about what they internalised—about themselves, their futures, and their worth.

Understanding debt as a story rather than just a statement is essential because it explains why so many repayment strategies fail—not due to mathematical error, but due to psychological resistance. If a person sees their debt as evidence of shame, failure, or incompetence, they are unlikely to approach it analytically. They avoid the account summary. They postpone the conversation. They minimise the problem publicly while privately agonising over it. In that sense, debt becomes not just a number, but an identity wound. The spreadsheet can't fix what the narrative has already corroded.

The roots of this narrative are often laid early. Many people inherit not just financial circumstances but *financial scripts*—unspoken beliefs absorbed in childhood. For some, it's the idea that debt is inherently immoral or a sign of irresponsibility. For others, it's that debt is inevitable, even necessary, to live a functional adult life. Others still are told, subtly or explicitly, that their value is tied to how well they can access credit, signal financial stability, or maintain consumer appearances. These scripts shape how people interpret borrowing: whether they see it as a tool, a trap, or a test of their maturity.

Consider the case of student loans. On paper, they are structured investments—borrow now, earn more later. But culturally, student debt has morphed into something heavier. It reflects a promise that didn't quite deliver. Graduates who did "all the right things"—studied hard, enrolled in university, took on loans to fund their education—now find themselves with degrees that may not yield the earnings they were led to expect. The result isn't just disillusionment with the education system. It's a deep sense of betrayal that rewires the borrower's relationship to financial risk. Many stop trusting themselves to make big financial decisions at all.

Credit card debt offers another layer to the story. It rarely begins as reckless spending. More often, it starts as an act of temporary survival: covering rent during a low-income month, paying for car repairs that couldn't wait, or funding a move in pursuit of better work. But once the balance grows, the emotional overlay intensifies. The borrower begins to feel that their financial life is no longer theirs. Interest accrues like a tax on time. Small expenses begin to feel dangerous. Future dreams are downgraded or deferred. Slowly, they stop seeing themselves as someone who could ever be debt-free—not because it's financially impossible, but because the story has calcified into a character: *I am someone who lives in debt.*

This self-concept is rarely challenged by mainstream financial advice. Most financial content is built for people who are already resourced with emotional clarity and cognitive bandwidth. It assumes that people make poor financial decisions because they lack information. But debt rarely exists in an information vacuum. It exists in emotional environments: under stress, shame, confusion, or inertia. A person who has learned to fear financial visibility will not spontaneously start budgeting just because a money coach told them to. They need to address the narrative first—*what does this debt mean to me? What does it say about who I am? What future do I believe is still available to me with this weight on my back?*

These questions matter because the story we believe shapes the behaviour we repeat. A person who sees themselves as perpetually behind is more likely to engage in scarcity thinking—avoiding long-term planning, overreacting to minor financial disruptions, and underspending on high-leverage investments like education, skills, or relocation. By contrast, someone who reclaims their debt narrative—who sees their debt not as a defining flaw but as a temporary configuration—can begin making proactive decisions: refinancing, prioritising high-interest repayments, or negotiating payment plans without the cloud of personal shame.

Changing this narrative requires more than positive affirmations. It demands an honest audit of what beliefs currently govern your financial behaviour. Do you believe you must work yourself to exhaustion to deserve financial peace? Do you believe that being debt-free is only for people who were born into privilege? Do you believe that paying off your debt means you must sacrifice joy, creativity, or identity along the way? These are not irrational thoughts—they are protective strategies built in response to lived experience. But once identified, they can be rewritten.

Rewriting the debt story does not mean denying responsibility. It means shifting the lens from self-blame to self-leadership. It allows you to ask not "What did I do wrong?" but "What system was I operating in—and how do I step outside of it without imploding my life?" This is not just a financial act, but a psychological one. It involves reconnecting with your capacity to choose, to strategise, to act—not out of guilt, but out of clarity.

This is especially relevant in a culture that both stigmatises debt and depends on it. Modern economies are structurally indebted: governments, corporations, and households all operate on borrowed capital. And yet, individuals—especially younger people—are expected to manage their debts with a kind of stoic perfectionism that ignores the complexity of real life. The contradiction is stark: we are trained to pursue degrees, homes, or business ventures through credit, but are then culturally punished for the financial outcomes of those choices if they fall short.

What's needed is not just financial literacy, but *narrative literacy*—the ability to identify and edit the stories we've inherited or absorbed. This may involve working with a financial therapist, journaling your debt beliefs, or simply speaking openly with trusted peers about the emotions that debt triggers. The goal is not to feel perfect about debt, but to feel *conscious*. Because once you are conscious, you can act. You can reframe the situation not as a moral verdict but as a solvable equation influenced by context, timing, and available tools.

Debt is neither inherently bad nor inherently disempowering. What makes it toxic is when it becomes a silent contract—one you never consented to but live under every day. To break that spell, you must see the debt not only as a number to eliminate but as a narrative to interrogate. You must move from a posture of shame to a posture of authorship. This is not about erasing the debt overnight. It is about changing what the debt means, how it functions in your psyche, and what future it allows you to imagine.

And that, more than any interest rate, is what determines your trajectory. Not just how much you owe, but *who you believe you are while owing it.* Debt, in that light, becomes not a verdict, but a prompt. And with the right tools, insight, and permission, it can become the opening line to a very different story—one authored by you.

The Shame Loop That Keeps You Stuck-

Shame doesn't just visit your finances—it moves in, redecorates, and changes the locks. It's not simply a reaction to a mistake; it becomes the lens through which every financial decision is interpreted. You don't just overspend—you see yourself as irresponsible. You're not just behind on payments—you start believing you're fundamentally incapable. In this way, shame isn't a symptom of poor financial health. It's a driver of it. Left unchecked, it hijacks decision-making, warps self-assessment, and entrenches people in cycles of avoidance, paralysis, or overcorrection. It's not the debt itself that breaks most people—it's the story they've been told, or told themselves, about what that debt says about who they are.

To understand the mechanics of the shame loop, we need to be precise. Shame is not the same as guilt. Guilt is adaptive; it signals that an action was misaligned with your values and can motivate corrective behaviour. Shame, by contrast, makes the issue personal. It says: *you didn't make a bad financial decision—you are a bad decision-maker.* Over time, this belief metastasises. You stop trusting yourself. You stop looking at your bank balance. You delay opening letters. You avoid discussions about money not because you're indifferent, but because every interaction confirms a distorted identity: *I'm not good with money, and I probably never will be.*

This distortion has real economic consequences. Financial shame reduces visibility, and visibility is foundational to improvement. If you can't look at the reality of your spending, debt, or earnings without spiralling into self-judgment, then you cannot plan rationally. Instead of examining the numbers, people operate off fear-based assumptions: *I'm probably too far gone. I wouldn't even know where to start. Even if I tried, I'd mess it up.* This emotional fog leads to short-term coping strategies that create long-term damage—minimum payments, impulse spending, hiding purchases, or swinging between over-control and total disengagement.

The shame loop is particularly common among people who were raised in environments where financial competence was moralised. If you grew up in a household where money was always tight, but appearances had to be maintained, you likely received mixed messages: money is private, but you should have more of it; being broke is not your fault, but you should feel ashamed; debt is normal, but talking about it is not. These contradictions become internalised. You learn to perform confidence while carrying fear. You strive for financial improvement while sabotaging the habits that would enable it—because deep down, you've confused punishment with responsibility.

Shame also thrives in silence. It feeds on secrecy and isolation. The less you speak about it, the more it shapes your inner world. The financial industry rarely helps here. Much personal finance advice assumes a neutral emotional baseline: that people will budget logically, pay off debt systematically, and adjust their behaviour in response to numeric feedback. But humans don't work that way under shame. Shame interrupts the feedback loop by distorting perception. A late payment isn't just a missed deadline—it's another confirmation that *you can't get your life together.* This emotional overcharge makes it nearly impossible to engage with money as a tool rather than a judgment.

To break this loop, clarity is not enough. You also need *compassionate permission.* Permission to look honestly at the numbers without letting them collapse your self-worth. Permission to feel regret without assuming ruin. Permission to change strategies without interpreting it as failure. This shift doesn't come from motivation hacks or punitive spreadsheets—it comes from narrative reconstruction. You must decouple your net worth from your self-worth. You must understand that debt, overspending, or lack of savings are outcomes—not verdicts. And outcomes can be changed with strategy, not self-flagellation.

Take, for example, a mid-career professional who earns well but carries persistent credit card debt. On paper, the fix is clear: restructure spending, increase payments, automate transfers. But emotionally, the issue is more complex. They may be carrying unresolved family dynamics—perhaps they were the first to "make it" financially and feel pressure to support others. Or perhaps money was a source of control or neglect in their upbringing, and spending has become a coping mechanism for stress, loneliness, or resentment. Without addressing those emotional undercurrents, the debt may decrease temporarily but return in a different form. The shame loop is not broken by better advice—it's broken by better self-understanding.

Another form of the shame loop is hyper-frugality. Some people react to financial missteps with excessive control: rigid budgets, guilt over small purchases, or complete avoidance of "non-essential" spending. This, too, is a reaction to shame—an attempt to prove worth through discipline. But hyper-control often masks fear. It doesn't build a healthier relationship with money; it just creates a new prison. Financial well-being isn't measured by how little you spend—it's measured by how aligned your spending is with your values, and how empowered you feel in the process.

A powerful antidote to shame is specificity. Vague feelings like "I'm terrible with money" must be translated into concrete questions: *What exactly is not working? What decision do I keep repeating? What am I afraid of?* This deconstructs the shame narrative and turns it into an actionable diagnostic. From there, you can engage with tools like spending audits, cash flow mapping, or financial therapy—not as punishments, but as clarifying practices. These tools won't work if they're used to reinforce self-blame. They work only when they're grounded in the belief that your value is stable—even when your finances are not.

Shame also thrives on comparison. Social media has intensified this. People are now constantly exposed to curated portrayals of financial success—debt-free journeys, six-figure businesses, passive income portfolios. But what's rarely visible are the support systems, inherited privileges, or mental health costs that shape those outcomes. When comparison replaces context, shame blooms. The belief that "everyone else has it together but me" becomes an emotional tax that saps the energy needed to actually improve. The key is not to eliminate aspiration—but to *anchor it in truth.* Financial progress must be defined on your terms, not by aesthetic or algorithm.

It's worth underscoring that shame is not only an individual burden—it's also a systemic tool. Institutions rely on shame to discourage transparency. Credit systems penalise those who speak up. Workplaces rarely provide financial literacy, but expect employees to manage retirement contributions and debt repayment seamlessly. Governments outsource financial risk to individuals—through student loans, medical debt, or underfunded pensions—

then shame them for struggling. Recognising the structural origins of financial shame doesn't absolve personal responsibility, but it does contextualise it. You are not broken. You are navigating a system designed without your full humanity in mind.

To exit the shame loop, you don't need to feel confident. You need to feel *curious*. Curiosity allows you to ask questions without self-judgment: *Why do I avoid looking at my statements? What emotion comes up when I think about saving? Where did I first learn that spending equals safety?* These are not soft questions—they are surgical. They reveal the architecture of your money beliefs. And once you see the architecture, you can begin to rebuild.

There is no perfect time to do this work. Waiting for full emotional readiness is itself part of the shame loop. The truth is, you become ready by starting—not the other way around. Small acts of financial visibility—checking your balance, opening a bill, tracking a day's worth of spending—can begin to undo years of avoidance. But only if they're done without internal punishment. That's the pivot point: not just doing the work, but changing the emotional context in which the work is done.

Shame convinces you that you must fix everything before you can feel good about yourself. But the paradox is this: it's only when you begin to feel good about yourself that you gain the clarity and courage to start fixing things. Financial change, then, is not just about tactics—it's about reclaiming emotional agency. It's about deciding that your past decisions, however flawed, do not disqualify you from future competence. And that real responsibility does not come from shame—it comes from belief. Belief that you are still the kind of person who can get clear, take action, and move forward—not because you've never made mistakes, but because you've learned not to make them mean more than they must.

Choosing the Right Debt Exit Strategy-

There's an often-missed truth about debt: the mechanics are universal, but the best exit is personal. Two people can owe the same amount, carry the same interest rates, and have identical incomes—

and yet require completely different strategies to get out. Why? Because debt doesn't exist in a vacuum. It intersects with temperament, habits, cash flow, risk tolerance, and—most critically—psychology. Paying off debt isn't simply a mathematical problem; it's an identity process. And that means choosing the "right" strategy has less to do with spreadsheets and more to do with aligning tactics to mindset.

Debt repayment frameworks—like avalanche, snowball, and hybrid methods—are often presented as interchangeable tools. In truth, they function more like lenses through which people see momentum. The avalanche method prioritises interest efficiency: pay off the highest-rate debts first to minimise long-term cost. The snowball method prioritises motivation: pay off the smallest balances first to feel quick wins and build emotional traction. The hybrid approach blends the two—anchoring early wins in psychology while still respecting long-term financial logic.

Each approach has merit. But none should be adopted blindly. The first task is not choosing the most "rational" strategy. It's *understanding the emotional terrain* you're navigating.

Let's start with the avalanche method. On paper, it is the most financially optimal route. High-interest debts—like credit cards or payday loans—drain wealth quickly, and tackling them first means less money lost to compounding fees. But the avalanche's efficiency can come at a psychological cost. If your largest debt also happens to carry the highest interest rate, it may take months—sometimes years—before you see meaningful progress. For highly analytical or emotionally steady individuals, this delay isn't an issue. For others, especially those recovering from financial shame or inertia, it can be demoralising. Progress that remains invisible is progress that's easy to abandon.

The snowball method offers a sharp contrast. By knocking out the smallest balances first, you build visible momentum. You prove to yourself that you can finish things. Each cleared account becomes a small psychological victory—proof that traction is possible. Critics of the snowball method argue that it sacrifices efficiency for emotion. That's true, but incomplete. *Behavioural consistency is more valuable than theoretical precision.* If snowballing balances builds enough confidence to keep you engaged, then the "extra" interest paid is not waste—it's the cost of sustained behavioural engagement.

Hybrid strategies attempt to reconcile the two. You may clear a small balance or two to gain traction, then shift your focus to high-interest accounts. Or you may split your repayment budget—putting a majority toward the highest interest debt, while directing a smaller amount to knock out a nuisance balance that's draining mental bandwidth. This approach respects both the numbers and the human behind them. It also acknowledges that strategies must be flexible. What works in month one may not be what sustains you in month twelve.

That said, choosing a strategy isn't merely about the structure of your debts—it's also about the structure of your life. Someone with highly variable income (such as a freelancer or gig worker) will approach debt differently than someone on a salaried contract. When your income fluctuates, prioritising liquidity and emergency reserves may take precedence over aggressive repayment. In such cases, it may be more prudent to pay minimums across all debts while building a cash buffer. This isn't procrastination—it's triage. *The stability of your financial system matters as much as its speed of resolution.*

Another key consideration is emotional regulation. Debt, for many, is not just a financial stressor but an emotional trigger. If your debt load creates anxiety, shame, or avoidance, your repayment plan must address more than dollars and cents—it must reduce volatility in your nervous system. That may mean setting up automatic minimum payments, using visual progress trackers, or building in occasional "spending allowances" to prevent burnout. An all-or-nothing repayment sprint often ends in collapse. A sustainable rhythm—paced, adaptive, and psychologically attuned—leads to longer-lasting freedom.

It's also worth examining the *origin* of the debt. This isn't always comfortable, but it's vital. Debt acquired for education, medical emergencies, or supporting family carries different emotional weight than debt accumulated through impulse purchases or lifestyle inflation. One isn't more legitimate than the other, but recognising the story behind the debt can clarify your approach. If your borrowing was survival-driven, your plan may need to account for emotional healing and support systems. If it was driven by lifestyle habits, your plan must include behavioural audits and value realignment—otherwise, you'll pay it off only to rebuild it.

Let's bring this into a practical context. Consider two individuals: one is a software engineer earning £70,000 per year, carrying £15,000 in credit card debt across three cards. The other is a retail manager earning £32,000 with £10,000 in personal loans and £5,000 in student overdraft. The engineer may benefit most from an avalanche strategy—targeting the card with 24% APR while maintaining minimums elsewhere. Their high disposable income means they can reduce principal rapidly and avoid heavy interest charges. The retail manager, however, may feel overwhelmed by the mental noise of managing multiple debts. A snowball approach—clearing the overdraft, then tackling the personal loan—could provide relief, clarity, and confidence. Even if the interest costs are slightly higher, the reduction in stress and confusion may justify it.

Both cases highlight the central insight: *the "right" strategy is the one you'll actually follow*. Debt freedom is not an exam to pass—it's a condition to design around your psychology, obligations, and aspirations.

A frequent point of confusion is whether to invest while paying off debt. This introduces a tension between mathematical optimisation and psychological payoff. From a strict numbers perspective, if your debt interest rate exceeds your investment return, you should prioritise the debt. But humans don't live in spreadsheets. Investing—even small amounts—can help build a parallel narrative: that you are not just correcting mistakes, but building a future. For some, this dual approach is motivating; for others, it splits focus and impedes traction. There's no universal answer. But the question must be asked *not* just in terms of financial return, but in terms of emotional reward and behavioural sustainability.

Another layer is how your debt strategy aligns with your broader financial identity. If you see yourself as someone building autonomy, does your plan reinforce that self-concept? Or does it feel punitive, endless, and draining? Strategy must serve identity—not just objectives. Debt payoff plans that feel oppressive often fail, not because they're flawed mathematically, but because they contradict your core aspirations. Your strategy should not merely be about erasing numbers—it should be about *building belief* in your competence and capability.

Many people fail to factor in emotional cash flow. Just as financial cash flow dictates whether you can meet expenses without borrowing, emotional cash flow determines whether you have the attention, energy, and self-trust to stick to a plan under stress. If your strategy ignores this bandwidth—if it expects you to make daily micro-decisions in a state of depletion—it will eventually collapse, even if it "should" have worked. The best strategy *simplifies your system.* It creates fewer points of friction, reduces decision fatigue, and builds rhythm.

For this reason, automation is not just a convenience—it's a discipline device. Automating payments enforces consistency while removing the need for repeated willpower. But it must be paired with regular visibility. If you automate everything but never review your progress, you risk disengagement. This is why pairing automation with a monthly financial check-in—fifteen minutes of reviewing your repayment progress, updating balances, and noting small wins—can amplify effectiveness. Progress feels slow until it's measured. Momentum grows where it's observed.

Lastly, exit strategy does not mean martyrdom. You do not have to eliminate all joy or flexibility to pay off debt. The plan that sacrifices all quality of life is rarely sustainable. Instead, *integrate restoration into your strategy.* If repaying £800 per month is possible but leaves you emotionally exhausted, consider repaying £700 and allocating £100 toward something life-giving—a hobby, self-education, or an experience. This doesn't delay progress—it protects it. Guilt-led deprivation rarely leads to freedom. Values-led consistency does.

Debt is not just a financial state—it's a negotiation between your present and future selves. The strategy you choose should reflect that complexity. It should not only move you forward mathematically, but build the internal foundation—clarity, stability, belief—that ensures you never have to return. Paying off debt isn't just about closing balances. It's about opening capacity—for agency, for vision, and for the kind of life that no longer needs permission from past mistakes to move forward.

Future-Facing Credit Habits-

Credit is often framed in starkly limited terms—either as a burden to be avoided or a score to be gamed. But both of these narratives miss the larger point: *credit is not just a record of your past; it's a lever for your future.* Whether your long-term goals include home ownership, launching a business, or building a life in a new country, your ability to use credit wisely will influence not only your options, but your confidence in pursuing them. This chapter is not about maximising points or hacking algorithms. It's about cultivating a credit philosophy that reflects self-trust, long-range vision, and intelligent constraint.

To do that, we must begin by redefining what credit actually is. It is not free money. Nor is it inherently dangerous. Credit is *a measurement of how the financial system interprets your behaviour under pressure.* A high credit score signals that you consistently follow through on obligations, use borrowed funds responsibly, and maintain stable financial routines. But the number itself is not the goal. *The goal is the capacity to borrow affordably and purposefully, when and if it accelerates your aspirations.*

This means that responsible credit use is less about constantly borrowing and more about curating a trustworthy financial identity over time. The paradox is that you must sometimes use credit to demonstrate that you don't depend on it. This is why one of the simplest habits—using a credit card regularly for small, planned expenses and paying it off in full each month—remains one of the most effective long-term strategies. It builds payment history, maintains active accounts, and keeps utilisation low without accumulating interest. It's not glamorous, but *discipline over drama builds durable leverage.*

But foundational habits alone aren't sufficient if they lack context. What matters is *how those habits compound into opportunity*. Consider the difference between someone with a 740 credit score who never borrows and someone with a 740 who uses credit strategically: to secure a low-interest mortgage, to qualify for a business line of credit, or to access favourable terms on relocation or visa sponsorship. Both people may be numerically identical on paper, but the second person is *credit-active*, not just *credit-compliant*. That distinction matters. Because having good credit isn't the same as *using credit well*.

Future-facing credit habits begin with this philosophical orientation: credit should support your autonomy, not subsidise your avoidance. That means using credit not to mask shortfalls or indulge impulse, but to amplify intentional decisions—such as consolidating higher-interest debt, investing in your own education, or building infrastructure that supports your next move professionally or geographically.

The distinction between constructive credit and compensatory credit is not semantic. It is behavioural. Constructive credit is purpose-driven, pre-planned, and bounded by exit strategies. Compensatory credit is reactive, vague, and emotionally charged. It surfaces when people are trying to solve internal tension with external borrowing: boredom, status anxiety, fear of missing out, or crisis management without a backup plan. The former builds your capacity. The latter often undermines it.

Building habits around constructive credit begins with data literacy. You need to know *how* your credit score is calculated—not to manipulate it, but to respect the logic behind it. The five pillars—payment history, utilisation, age of accounts, credit mix, and new inquiries—are not arbitrary. They reflect behavioural signals. The system is asking: do you pay reliably? Do you avoid maxing out your limits? Do you manage longstanding relationships with creditors? Do you handle different types of debt (e.g., revolving vs instalment)? And do you apply for new credit sparingly?

Once you understand this, you can approach your finances like an architect rather than a borrower. For instance, keeping your credit utilisation below 30% of available limits sends a strong signal of restraint—even if you can technically afford to carry more. Similarly, maintaining older accounts—even those you rarely use—can improve your score by extending your average account age. And resisting unnecessary credit checks (especially within short timeframes) preserves your score from unnecessary dings. These are not tricks. They're design choices. *Every habit you form today builds a future that either expands or constricts your options.*

But even these mechanical elements are not enough if they're divorced from values. You must tie your credit decisions to the life you're actively designing. Let's say your vision includes moving to another country in five years. That vision should shape how you manage credit today: avoiding excessive debt, ensuring credit cards are manageable across borders, building strong repayment history to increase the likelihood of international financial institutions or immigration authorities viewing you as low-risk. Or suppose you're planning to start a business in two years. A good credit history can open access to lower-interest business loans, personal credit lines, or even partnerships with vendors who trust your payment track record. *Good credit is often a silent prerequisite for opportunity.*

That's also why credit should be treated with intentionality—not shame. Many people who have struggled with debt or defaulted in the past develop a defensive relationship to credit. They become either overly fearful—avoiding all forms of borrowing—or overly indifferent, assuming their record has already disqualified them from meaningful opportunity. Both responses are understandable, but neither is optimal. The truth is that credit history is more malleable than many assume. Late payments, collections, and defaults lose their weight over time. Strategic rebuilding—through secured cards, responsible repayment, and limited inquiries—can significantly restore trustworthiness within two to three years. The system is designed to reward *recent discipline*, not punish *distant errors.*

Still, rebuilding requires more than clean mechanics. It requires a psychological shift—from performing penance to exercising sovereignty. This means you don't just "pay off debt" or "avoid credit." You *take command* of your narrative. You define what your credit is for. That might mean rejecting credit card offers that don't serve your lifestyle, or choosing credit products with no foreign transaction fees because your five-year plan includes global mobility. It might mean declining to co-sign a loan that exposes you to unnecessary risk—even if your credit score could "handle it." *Credit responsibility includes saying no, not just managing yes.*

The final layer of future-facing credit behaviour is proactive visibility. Many people treat credit like a fire alarm: they check it only when something goes wrong. This approach keeps them reactive and uninformed. Instead, treat your credit file as part of your monthly audit. Monitor your credit report for errors, understand your interest rates and terms, and remain alert to changing eligibility requirements for financial products tied to major goals. For instance, if you plan to buy property in three years, learning now what credit thresholds lenders require enables you to prepare deliberately rather than scramble later. *Credit awareness allows you to act before your circumstances demand it.*

Technology can help. There are now tools that simulate how specific actions—like paying down balances or opening new accounts—affect your credit profile. Used correctly, these tools reinforce strategic thinking. Used impulsively, they enable score-chasing behaviour that misses the point. The most valuable use of credit tools is not to increase your number by ten points for the sake of ego, but to test whether your behaviours today support the financial moves you'll need tomorrow.

That is ultimately the essence of future-facing credit habits: *a series of deliberate behaviours aligned with long-term self-determination.* Not obedience to arbitrary rules. Not avoidance driven by past mistakes. But principled, aware, and flexible use of a tool that—when mastered—can dramatically accelerate the architecture of your goals.

Your credit should be a reflection of your clarity, not your confusion. A record of priorities, not pressures. A score, yes—but more importantly, a story. A story of reliability, restraint, and readiness for whatever future you're building toward.

Chapter 5
Design a Personal Money System

There persists a pervasive myth in personal finance: that success is a matter of sheer willpower—the fortitude to skip small pleasures, the stamina to monitor every transaction, the self-restraint to resist every fleeting impulse. This idea, however, is not only outdated; it misunderstands the architecture of human behaviour. The most financially resilient individuals are rarely those with the strongest discipline. They are those with the clearest systems—structures that determine the flow of money before emotions can intervene. Systems that translate objectives into defaults, making consistency almost inevitable and self-sabotage increasingly unlikely.

This chapter is less about budgeting and more about design. Specifically, the construction of a personal money system that aligns with your psychology, your values, and your long-term ambitions—without demanding constant vigilance or emotional energy. The focus is structural rather than moral: no guilt, no shaming, just mechanics. How can your environment be crafted so that better financial behaviour occurs naturally, without relying on heroic self-control?

The distinction between motivation and infrastructure is crucial. Most people stumble not from lack of discipline, but from systems that demand endless micro-decisions. Each time money enters an account, questions arise: How much should I save? What can I spend? May I treat myself? Should I feel guilty if I do? This continual decision-making drains cognitive resources and erodes self-trust. But once a well-calibrated system is in place, decisions are made upstream, allowing behaviour to flow downstream almost automatically.

The foundational principle is simple: systems outperform intentions over time. Behavioural economics bears this out. Humans predictably forget, procrastinate, rationalise, or drift—especially under stress, or when rewards feel distant. Systems, thoughtfully designed, bypass these frailties. This is true not only for money, but for diet, exercise, learning, and leadership. The patterns that endure are those that reduce friction for desired behaviour and increase friction for counterproductive choices.

Applying this to finances begins with a deceptively simple structure: the three-account framework. This is not a repackaged 50/30/20 rule, but a flexible scaffolding for clarity, built around three functions: stability, flexibility, and growth. One account covers predictable living costs. Another is reserved for discretionary spending that enhances quality of life. The third is strictly for long-term positioning—saving, investing, and building leverage. This model works across earnings levels and employment types, accommodating the volatility of freelancers, the regularity of salaried workers, and the cash-flow rhythms of business owners alike.

Yet even architecture must be reinforced with automation. Systems succeed not by will alone, but by passively shaping behaviour. Direct deposit splits, standing orders, and scheduled transfers pre-allocate funds before the temptation to misallocate arises. Behavioural science calls this "choice architecture": you remove poor options entirely, leaving monitoring rather than constant decision-making as your role. This is how financial systems scale—through reduction of noise, not force of will.

Acknowledging that one size does not fit all, the chapter introduces the anti-budget. For those fatigued by rigid categories or overwhelmed by spreadsheets—particularly neurodivergent readers—this model offers freedom. The anti-budget tracks a single variable: what remains after essential goals are funded. Define what matters first—retirement, travel, or a buffer—then use the remainder freely, without guilt or overthinking. The principle is simple: handle the hard part upfront, and reclaim permission to engage with money consciously rather than reactively.

Systems exist within ecosystems. Yet few audit the total environment: banks, platforms, subscriptions, apps, and even advice networks. Are they creating clarity or friction? Do they reinforce trust in your decisions, or distract with complexity? Are your advisors aligned with your vision, or merely projecting their own unresolved narratives? A full ecosystem audit surfaces these influences, revealing gaps and misalignments. The goal is coherence, not perfection; every element should support the direction of your chosen future.

Underpinning all of this is a critical truth: fewer real-time decisions mean more mental energy for what matters. A system does not merely manage money—it liberates attention. In a world engineered to monetise distraction, reclaiming attention is one of the most valuable gains imaginable.

This chapter does not claim that a three-account framework or anti-budget resolves every financial challenge. It offers something more profound: a shift from improvisation to intentionality, from scrambling to planning, from tracking mistakes to designing defaults. The aim is not to mechanise your financial life, but to engineer scaffolding that supports your best instincts consistently—without exhausting your willpower.

Ultimately, a personal money system is not a template to copy. It is a reflection of how you think clearly about your priorities, your values, and your long-term goals. It only functions if you make it your own.

Systems Over Willpower-

Most people overestimate their willpower and underestimate their environment. They assume that if they just tried harder—if they were more disciplined, more committed, more focused—they would finally get their finances under control. This belief is comforting because it places the solution squarely within reach. But it is also misleading. *Discipline is not a sustainable strategy—structure is.* Long-term financial success doesn't come from trying harder each day; it comes from designing systems that make the right actions automatic and the wrong ones harder to access.

Willpower is a limited cognitive resource. Numerous studies in behavioural psychology, including those by Roy Baumeister and Kathleen Vohs, have demonstrated that willpower depletes with use. The more decisions we have to make—what to eat, what to wear, whether to save or spend—the more likely we are to default to convenience, emotional gratification, or inaction. This is called decision fatigue, and it plays a quiet but powerful role in personal finance. People don't overspend because they lack character; they overspend because they're mentally exhausted by the time they confront a choice that demands restraint.

Nowhere is this more evident than in the structure of modern consumer life. The average person is exposed to thousands of marketing messages per day. Every swipe, scroll, or tap contains embedded nudges designed to monetise your attention and fracture your impulse control. If your financial stability depends on saying no to every digital temptation, you are playing a game that was engineered for you to lose.

The antidote is not guilt. It is architecture. Financial systems—when well-designed—function like behavioural scaffolding. They pre-empt poor decisions by shaping your defaults. For instance, if your income is automatically routed into purpose-defined accounts the moment it arrives, the emotional debate about how much to save becomes irrelevant. If subscriptions are reviewed quarterly on a calendar invite, you don't need to rely on memory or motivation. *Systems replace discipline with design.* They are upstream solutions to downstream problems.

Consider the difference between someone who tries to budget manually every month versus someone who sets up a fixed standing order to transfer 20% of income into a separate investment account before they ever see it. The first person must decide, repeatedly, how much to save and whether to override competing temptations. The second has made one decision—once—and the system executes it silently in the background. Over years, this difference becomes not just behavioural but transformational. *Tiny structural advantages compound.*

This principle applies across contexts. Take food: if you stock your kitchen with whole ingredients instead of processed snacks, you don't need to summon willpower to eat healthily—you've designed away the worst options. In exercise: if your gym bag is packed and placed by the door, the resistance to going drops dramatically. The same logic governs money. Your environment either amplifies your intentions or undermines them. And if it isn't helping you, it's hurting you. There is no neutral financial infrastructure—only systems that serve your goals or systems that siphon from them.

But structure must be personalised. One-size-fits-all financial systems often fail because they ignore context. A 25-year-old freelance designer with variable income cannot copy the habits of a salaried manager with predictable cash flow. The solution lies in adapting principles to circumstance. For example, instead of rigid budgeting, a freelancer might benefit more from percentage-based allocations that flex in proportion to their monthly earnings. Income comes in, 60% goes to essentials, 20% to taxes, 10% to investments, and 10% to discretionary spending. No tracking every pound—just an elegant system that evolves in scale but not in logic.

Automation is a critical lever. When used intentionally, it minimises cognitive load and reduces the chance of error. Automatic savings plans, recurring investments, bill pay scheduling—these are not just conveniences, they are behavioural anchors. They allow your financial life to keep moving in the right direction even when your emotional state or energy level isn't cooperating. *Automation protects your future self from your present self's inconsistency.*

Critically, though, a system should never become a straightjacket. The goal is to build frameworks that are responsive, not rigid. You should be able to adapt your system as your goals evolve, your income grows, or your responsibilities shift. This is especially important for people managing multiple roles—caregivers, students, entrepreneurs—where predictability is often a luxury. Flexibility must be engineered into the design. Think: dynamic guardrails, not hard walls.

One useful diagnostic is to ask: *Does my current system require me to think about money constantly, or does it help me think about money clearly and less often?* If you are constantly budgeting, recalculating, and justifying every transaction, you are not operating a system—you are improvising. A true system creates clarity and reduces noise. It gives you permission to zoom out, focus on meaningful work, and trust that the essentials are being handled in the background.

But there is a cultural tension at play here. We live in a society that glorifies hustle and equates struggle with virtue. "No pain, no gain" is still treated as financial gospel. The idea of building a life that feels smooth, elegant, and low-friction is often misread as laziness. This is nonsense. Systems are not an escape from effort—they are a refinement of it. They take the most important, high-leverage behaviours and turn them into defaults, so that your energy can be redirected toward creativity, strategy, and growth. *Simplicity is not the absence of rigour—it is its highest form.*

We should also confront the moral undertones often embedded in personal finance advice. Many teachings assume that if you're struggling financially, it's because you haven't worked hard enough, sacrificed enough, or tracked enough. Rarely do they acknowledge the structural realities: income volatility, systemic bias, predatory financial products, or the invisible tax of chronic stress. Designing systems isn't about bypassing these forces—it's about reclaiming control in spite of them. It is a form of self-respect. It says: I will not leave my future to chance or my daily decisions to fatigue.

Real-world systems don't need to be elaborate. A colour-coded bank account structure, a simple spreadsheet reviewed every fortnight, or a calendar invite to revisit goals quarterly—these are systems. A folder of pre-approved purchases to minimise impulse buys. A friend you text each time you hit a savings milestone. These are also systems. The test is not complexity, but consistency. *Does the system reduce friction and improve alignment? Does it work even when you're distracted, tired, or anxious?*

There's also a deeper benefit. Systems build self-trust. When you consistently follow through—not because you remembered, but because you architected the process—you begin to see yourself as reliable. That identity shift changes everything. It reduces guilt, improves decision-making, and gives you momentum. And momentum is arguably the most underappreciated asset in personal finance. Once systems are humming, the need for motivation drops off almost entirely. You begin to see results not from Herculean effort, but from elegance. That is the difference between trying to manage your money and actually owning your financial life.

Ultimately, the choice isn't between discipline and structure—it's between relying on will or designing for success. Willpower is reactive. It asks you to respond well in the moment. Systems are proactive. They assume you won't. And that is their genius. They respect your humanity by reducing your vulnerability. They translate your best intentions into everyday results. Not by demanding more effort, but by embedding clarity where chaos usually lives.

This is the future of personal finance: not tighter control, but better design. Not more hustle, but less friction. Systems over willpower—not because you are weak, but because you are smart enough to know that even your strongest day is no match for a well-designed default.

The 3-Account Framework-

Every income event is a decision point, whether acknowledged or not. The moment money enters your hands—or your account—it begins to flow, shaped by habits, heuristics, obligations, and unconscious biases. Without a structure, most people default to reactive financial behaviours: paying bills, covering immediate needs, maybe saving what's left. But *what's left* is rarely enough, and over time, this improvisational model collapses under the weight of misalignment. The antidote isn't a more detailed budget or tighter restriction. It's clarity through intentional structure. That's where the 3-Account Framework comes in: a simple yet powerful system designed not only to stabilise cash flow, but to actively promote freedom, flexibility, and future growth.

At its core, this model breaks income into three distinct but interrelated purposes. It re-engineers the flow of funds to ensure that each pound you earn supports not just present obligations, but long-term vision. The design is elegant: one account for *Freedom*, one for *Flexibility*, and one for *Future Growth*. Unlike conventional financial advice that often prescribes abstract ratios or moralises spending, this framework anchors behaviour in functional psychology. *It's less about "good" or "bad" spending, and more about spending that's contextually coherent with your evolving goals.*

Let's start with the *Freedom Account.* This is your operational base. It covers the essentials—rent or mortgage, utilities, groceries, transport, insurance, and any non-negotiable obligations. For most people, this represents the largest proportion of their income allocation, typically between 50% and 70%, depending on location and lifestyle. The point isn't austerity—it's predictability. When essentials are isolated in their own container, you immediately reduce cognitive friction. You know what's covered. You stop treating every transaction as a stress test. And that psychological buffer—knowing the basics are structurally secured—creates the emotional bandwidth necessary to make better decisions elsewhere.

The second pillar is the *Flexibility Account.* This is the one most people either mismanage or neglect. Flexibility covers the variable layer of life: dining out, holidays, gifts, entertainment, unexpected costs. But it's also the category where autonomy is developed. By allocating a distinct amount for discretionary use, you avoid the binary trap of indulgence versus guilt. You have permission to spend—*on purpose.* The amount varies based on income level, risk appetite, and personal priorities, but even 10% allocated here can dramatically shift your relationship with money. Spending becomes a choice, not a compulsion. And when the flexibility account hits zero, you're not "broke"—you're simply operating within a clear boundary.

Third is the *Future Growth Account.* This is where compounding lives—not just in a financial sense, but in identity and confidence. Funds here go toward long-term investments, retirement savings, personal development, business ventures, or upskilling. It's a vote for the person you're becoming. For W2 earners, this might be a pension contribution or a regular transfer into an investment ISA. For freelancers or business owners, it could be capital reserves, tax provisions, or self-funded sabbaticals for strategic learning. What matters is that money enters this account regularly, not as an afterthought but as a first-order priority. This is the account that funds not just survival or pleasure, but *progress.*

Why does this model outperform traditional budgeting for most people? Because it translates abstract goals into concrete flows. It acknowledges that people don't just need savings accounts—they need mental categories that align with their lived experience. Traditional budgets fail not because people are irresponsible, but because they demand constant tracking and don't accommodate the rhythm of real life. The 3-Account Framework builds in fluidity while preserving direction.

For salaried employees, implementation is straightforward. You set up standing orders to distribute your net income into the three accounts the moment it lands. For example, 60% to Freedom, 20% to Flexibility, 20% to Future Growth. These ratios can evolve, but the principle is fixed: structure first, emotion second. You spend from your Flexibility Account without shame, invest from your Growth Account without hesitation, and sleep knowing your essentials are covered.

Self-employed readers face more complexity—but also more opportunity. Income is variable. Expenses may spike irregularly. But that variability makes structure even more essential. The model expands slightly here: before the 3-Account system begins, revenue must pass through two preliminary filters—*Business Expenses* and *Tax Provisioning*. Only what's left—your actual take-home profit—feeds the framework. Once filtered, the same principles apply. This creates both protection and precision. You're not guessing what's safe to spend. You're operating from clean, pre-decided buckets. And that psychological clarity is often the difference between chronic anxiety and stable confidence.

Importantly, the 3-Account Framework doesn't fix every problem—but it reframes the right ones. It doesn't ask you to become a spreadsheet zealot. It doesn't punish you for buying coffee or taking holidays. Instead, it forces you to reconcile your money behaviour with your stated values. If you say long-term freedom matters, but nothing goes into Future Growth, the inconsistency becomes visible. That visibility is not shame—it's power. Systems don't require perfection; they require consistency and visibility. Over time, the alignment between structure and intention becomes a form of self-trust.

There are edge cases, of course. Someone living below the poverty line will not be able to distribute income in neat proportions. But even then, *clarity beats chaos*. Even allocating £10 a month into a Future Growth account isn't meaningless—it's symbolic momentum. And momentum matters more than precision when building habits. Conversely, high-income earners often fall into a different trap: they assume their earning power justifies loose structure. But the absence of constraint leads to lifestyle inflation and strategic drift. More income without more system usually leads to more waste, not more wealth.

One of the quiet virtues of this framework is that it externalises trade-offs. If your Flexibility Account is exhausted but your Freedom Account is stable, you're not in crisis—you just have to pause discretionary spending until the next cycle. No guilt. No overthinking. If your Future Growth allocation is underweight for two months, that's a signal—not a moral failing. The system becomes a dashboard, not a doctrine. It tells you where you are, and more importantly, where your attention needs to go next.

Technological tools can enhance the model. Most banks now offer sub-accounts or "spaces" that allow users to replicate the framework within a single platform. Apps like Monzo, Starling, or Revolut let you visualise categories and automate flows. For those who prefer analog methods, a simple spreadsheet or even envelope-based system works just as well. The sophistication of the tool is secondary to the clarity of intent.

Ultimately, what makes the 3-Account Framework powerful is not its novelty—it's its usability. It works across income levels, lifestyles, and employment models. It respects the messy realities of modern life while providing a compass toward stability and self-actualisation. And it liberates the individual from the tyranny of micro-decisions, replacing them with macro-alignment. You are not your impulses. You are not your bank balance. You are the architect of a system that reflects what you care about—and who you're becoming.

If financial freedom means anything, it must begin here: not with radical discipline or complex software, but with a structure so clear, it makes freedom feel inevitable. The 3-Account Framework doesn't promise perfection. It promises progress. And progress, sustained by structure, is the most reliable engine of financial transformation.

The Anti-Budget That Works-

The word *budget* is one of the most emotionally loaded in modern personal finance. For many, it triggers a sense of failure before the exercise even begins—an association with denial, deprivation, or yet another attempt at self-improvement destined to collapse under the weight of complexity. Traditional budgets ask you to track every pound, categorise every coffee, and project months in advance how much you'll spend on toothpaste. While well-intentioned, this framework assumes a level of consistency, foresight, and attention that is neither natural nor necessary for most people. Especially for neurodivergent individuals or those managing multiple life domains simultaneously, traditional budgeting creates *friction*—not clarity. The solution isn't to abandon financial awareness. It's to re-engineer the process around human psychology rather than around accounting theory.

This is where the Anti-Budget steps in—not as a rebellion against responsibility, but as a redesign of financial accountability itself. *It reverses the logic of budgeting entirely: instead of tracking every outflow, you pre-allocate key inflows and allow everything else to flow freely within safe boundaries.* It's a structure built not on control, but containment.

The basic premise is radical in its simplicity. Rather than micromanaging expenses across 20 categories, you automate the big wins up front—savings, investments, and fixed essentials—and then stop worrying about the rest. You create a system where your most important financial behaviours happen without needing willpower, spreadsheets, or constant decision-making. The goal is behavioural sustainability, not numerical perfection.

Consider a young professional earning £3,000 per month after tax. Instead of planning every expenditure, they set up automatic transfers at the start of the month: £600 to long-term savings and investments, £1,200 to rent and fixed bills, and the remaining £1,200 left in their spending account for everything else. No manual tracking. No daily guilt. Just containment. If that spending account runs low by the third week, it's a prompt for curiosity—not panic. Because their future is already funded and their obligations are already covered, they're not failing—they're learning.

This approach is particularly powerful for those with ADHD or executive function challenges, who often struggle with the constant friction of conventional budgeting. When every financial decision requires activation energy—opening an app, comparing receipts, updating a sheet—the system collapses under cognitive load. The Anti-Budget removes the bottleneck. By front-loading key priorities and then allowing fluidity within constraints, it gives structure without suffocation. *It aligns with how humans actually behave—not how we wish they would on a good day with infinite bandwidth.*

Critics of anti-budgeting often conflate it with laziness or avoidance. But this is a category error. Rigidity is not synonymous with discipline, and tracking is not the same as insight. Many people who meticulously record every expense remain misaligned with their values. They know where every pound goes but have no clarity on *why*. The Anti-Budget doesn't just reduce friction—it elevates purpose. It forces the hard decisions up front: What matters most? What will you automate? What are you willing to let go of micromanaging so you can focus on your priorities?

For example, a freelance designer might allocate 30% of their monthly revenue into a tax holding account, 20% into savings and reinvestment, 40% toward operational expenses, and keep the remaining 10% as flexible cash. They don't track how many oat lattes they buy. They don't spend hours each week reconciling purchases. They know that the structural commitments—the non-negotiables that move their life forward—are already handled. What remains is play, permission, and space. *And that psychological space often leads to better behaviour than any granular ledger ever could.*

The Anti-Budget is not anti-metrics—it's anti-friction. It can be layered with occasional reviews to track annual trends or identify creeping lifestyle inflation. It can coexist with financial dashboards or net worth trackers. But the day-to-day operations remain intentionally low-maintenance. This reduces burnout, which in turn increases adherence, which ultimately increases results. *The best financial system is not the one you admire; it's the one you actually follow.*

One of the more under-discussed strengths of this model is its ability to adapt over time. Traditional budgets often crumble during life transitions—starting a new job, moving cities, entering parenthood—because they demand constant recalibration. The Anti-Budget, by contrast, absorbs change more naturally. Because it operates at the level of flow rather than category, adjustments can be made quickly. Income increases? Adjust the percentages. New goal? Create a new automatic transfer. There's no need to reinvent the system—just redirect the streams.

Technology can enhance this model, but it is not essential. Many digital banks now offer functionality that aligns perfectly with anti-budgeting: Monzo's "pots," Starling's "spaces," or apps like YNAB (ironically rooted in budgeting) allow users to segment funds in a visual, frictionless way. But even a single current account paired with one or two scheduled standing orders can implement the core structure effectively. The tool is secondary. The mindset is primary.

That mindset hinges on a single principle: *front-load what matters, then stop obsessing over what doesn't.* This is the inverse of how most people operate—neglecting long-term priorities while agonising over £3 impulse purchases. The Anti-Budget flips this by embedding values into the flow of funds. Once the system is in place, you're free to live within its boundaries without performance anxiety. *It's less a financial tool than a behavioural scaffolding.*

Another benefit of the Anti-Budget is emotional neutrality. Many budgeting systems carry a moral undertone: spending on experiences is "bad," subscriptions are "wasteful," eating out is "irresponsible." But these judgements are context-dependent and often unhelpful. The Anti-Budget doesn't care whether you spent £150 on theatre tickets or tech gadgets last month. If you're allocating money toward future growth, handling obligations, and staying within your flexible boundaries, then your spending *is* aligned. That alignment—not purity—is the marker of maturity.

This also makes the framework inclusive. For neurodivergent individuals who experience time, planning, and energy differently, it offers a rare blend of control and compassion. It doesn't demand perfect executive function to stay on track. For high-performing professionals with no time for daily expense tracking, it creates clarity without clutter. And for anyone recovering from financial anxiety, burnout, or shame, it allows progress without reactivating trauma.

None of this is to suggest that detail-oriented budgets have no place. For individuals in crisis, trying to reverse debt spirals or regain situational awareness, granular tracking can be temporarily invaluable. But it should be seen as a *tool*, not an identity. Budgeting is a means to an end—financial alignment—not a virtue in itself. And once the awareness is built, transitioning to a more fluid model may be the very thing that preserves momentum.

To design your own Anti-Budget, begin with two simple questions: *What do I want to happen automatically every month, without effort or emotion?* And *how much of my money am I willing to spend freely, without guilt or tracking, once those core priorities are handled?* From there, the rest is logistics. You don't need a perfect formula. You need a default flow that reflects your values, absorbs your variability, and allows you to live without chronic vigilance.

Because at the heart of financial freedom is not just having enough money—but having enough mental space. The Anti-Budget offers that space. Not through passivity or avoidance, but through intentional simplification. You automate the hard parts so you can live the good parts. You protect your future without policing your present. And in a world increasingly optimised for distraction and noise, *a system that delivers clarity without exhaustion may be the most valuable investment you'll ever make.*

Your Financial Ecosystem-

Every financial life is shaped by more than income and expenses. It is constructed—often unconsciously—by the systems, interfaces, and relationships that mediate our money decisions. These form your *financial ecosystem*: the constellation of banks, apps, payment habits, defaults, technologies, service providers, and even conversations that either reinforce clarity or breed friction. Like a digital operating system for your money, it can either amplify your focus or erode it silently.

Most people inherit their ecosystem passively. They open a bank account at age 18 and never question it. They download whatever budgeting app a friend recommends, default to tap-to-pay for convenience, and adopt the money habits of their closest peers or family. Over time, their financial environment becomes a patchwork—half-designed, half-drifted into. The result? Decision fatigue, hidden inefficiencies, and a chronic feeling of disconnection from their own financial reality.

The environment we operate in shapes our behaviour more than the intentions we hold. Just as a cluttered kitchen undermines healthy eating, a scattered or opaque financial setup undermines financial confidence. If you have five bank accounts, seven subscriptions, two savings apps, a pile of unopened financial statements, and no central dashboard—you're not failing at money. You're trying to function inside a fragmented system.

The first step is recognising that no financial decision is ever made in a vacuum. Whether you're paying a bill, investing in a business, or deciding whether to upgrade your phone, your environment either accelerates clarity or impairs it. Consider the difference between someone who has automated transfers into distinct sub-accounts—labelled "rent," "emergency," and "freedom fund"—versus someone relying on memory and mental maths each week. The latter may feel in control, but they are consuming cognitive bandwidth every day. The former has outsourced discipline to structure.

This is why auditing your financial ecosystem is not a luxury—it's a necessity. An audit isn't about judgement. It's about surfacing design flaws so you can replace them with systems that serve you. Start by mapping what currently exists: every account, tool, and recurring financial relationship. Ask: What role does this serve? Does it reduce friction or add complexity? Does it reinforce my values or create noise?

Take banking, for instance. Many people use a single current account as a catch-all container for income, bills, savings, and discretionary spending. This makes cashflow opaque and planning almost impossible. Simply shifting to a multi-account setup—one for income, one for fixed costs, one for spending—can transform your relationship with money. Not because it adds complexity, but because it *adds visibility.*

Then look at subscriptions and services. Are you paying for convenience or out of inertia? Do the financial tools you use make you smarter or just busier? A premium budgeting app might be worthwhile if it provides clarity you act on—but a waste if it simply gamifies guilt. Likewise, paying a financial adviser makes sense when the service adds personalised insight, not if it simply maintains status quo with jargon.

Your digital habits matter too. Are you using multiple payment methods—debit cards, credit cards, BNPL platforms, digital wallets—without any integration? Do you receive important banking notifications buried among promotional emails? Is your financial life visible at a glance, or do you need to log into five platforms to understand your current state? *Confusion is expensive, and fragmentation compounds over time.*

But your ecosystem isn't just digital—it's relational. Think about the people who influence your financial thinking: friends, partners, colleagues, parents. Are these relationships expanding your financial range or reinforcing patterns you've outgrown? Are you in regular conversations about money that are grounded in curiosity, clarity, and ambition? Or are you operating in silence, anxiety, or performative competence? Sometimes, the most powerful shift in your financial ecosystem isn't an app—it's permission to rethink who you compare yourself to.

A healthy ecosystem should have *redundancy without chaos*. It should offer security, flexibility, and a clear map of where your money goes and why. That means tools for automation (so your goals move forward without daily effort), interfaces for insight (so you can track what matters), and a structure that reinforces your core values—not someone else's template. The system should bend around your life, not force you into someone else's rules.

Let's walk through a practical audit. Open a document and list out the core components of your financial life. Start with these:

– Income sources: Where does your money come from? Is it stable or variable? Do you have visibility on inflows week to week?
– Bank accounts: How many do you have? What is each one used for? Is your naming and structure intuitive or confusing?
– Payment platforms: Are you using Apple Pay, PayPal, Klarna, or credit facilities? Do you understand how each one affects your behaviour or credit score?
– Savings and investments: Where are they held? Are they allocated by goal or simply lumped together? Do you know the interest or return rates? Are they automated?
– Subscriptions and bills: What renews automatically? What's being paid for and never used? What's worth keeping but needs renegotiation?
– Financial apps and dashboards: Are you relying on spreadsheets, apps, or mental tracking? What gives you insight vs what distracts?
– Human relationships: Who do you regularly talk about money with? Who influences your choices? Who could you learn from or support more honestly?

Once you've mapped this, categorise each item as either *amplifying clarity* or *adding noise*. Anything in the latter category is a candidate for redesign. That doesn't mean cutting everything. It might mean repurposing an account, simplifying payment flows, or finally merging that old bank account you opened a decade ago for student loans.

This process doesn't have to happen all at once. You're not redesigning a corporation's treasury function. But even two or three meaningful tweaks—like consolidating accounts, setting up naming conventions, or shifting to a unified financial dashboard—can yield disproportionate results. The clarity that emerges from this cleanup isn't just administrative. It's psychological. *When you can see your system clearly, you can trust it. And when you trust it, you no longer have to live in a state of background financial anxiety.*

There's also a compounding effect to an optimised ecosystem. The fewer decisions you have to make each day, the more attention you can direct toward strategic thinking: launching a side business, investing with intention, exploring geographic arbitrage, or negotiating better contracts. When your system supports you instead of relying on you, you unlock time, confidence, and momentum.

The final layer of the ecosystem is optionality. A good system gives you the power to pivot. That means retaining access to emergency funds, understanding your liabilities, and maintaining buffers—not just in cash but in attention. An overwhelmed financial system might "work" in calm seasons but break instantly during change. A resilient one anticipates the unexpected. *Redundancy is not inefficiency; it's resilience by design.*

Designing your financial ecosystem isn't glamorous. There are no inspirational quotes or influencer reels that show someone reviewing banking interfaces at 10pm. But this invisible architecture is what underpins every visible outcome. It's the scaffolding that determines whether your goals accelerate or stall. And while the process may feel tedious at first, the result is anything but. What emerges is a life where money flows with less friction, where decisions feel grounded instead of reactive, and where clarity becomes your default state—not your monthly aspiration.

A messy system doesn't mean you're bad with money. It means your environment was never designed to support the way you actually live. When you change that environment—deliberately, compassionately, and structurally—you don't just improve your finances. *You reclaim your cognitive freedom, your emotional energy, and your strategic attention.* And from that place, far more becomes possible.

Chapter 6
Stack Income, Not Hustle

The glorification of the hustle has become something of a cultural reflex, an unspoken badge of honour equating exhaustion with virtue and perpetual busyness with ambition. It's woven into the language of side gigs, the aesthetics of grind culture, and the myth that working longer hours guarantees financial freedom. Yet for many chasing the next invoice, freelance client, or side project, the treadmill feels endless: the scenery changes, calendars fill, yet real financial elevation rarely follows. This chapter proposes an alternative: not to hustle harder, but to stack smarter.

Earning power does not correlate directly with effort; it is amplified through structure. Those who achieve both financial stability and creative fulfilment seldom log the longest hours. Instead, they cultivate leverage by stacking skills. They identify capabilities that compound—writing, design, strategy, coding, negotiation, communication—and arrange them to magnify value across roles and markets. This is the essence of income stacking: deliberately layering competencies to generate optionality, scalability, and resilience, shifting from selling time to building systems, assets, or ideas that return value beyond linear labour.

Consider two freelancers. One spends forty hours a week chasing clients, billing by the hour, and producing bespoke work from scratch each cycle. Another orchestrates a skill-based ecosystem: consulting three days a week, licensing a template or course, running a newsletter that generates affiliate revenue, and managing a quarterly cohort-based programme. The first works harder; the second earns more. The difference is not hustle—it is design.

Design begins by escaping what might be called the grind loop: a behavioural trap where activity masquerades as progress. The grind loop is seductive because it rewards the illusion of productivity, flattering the ego with action while quietly draining strategic focus. Exhausted, you default to what feels immediately productive, and your earning potential plateaus—not from lack of effort, but from lack of elevation.

Income stacking introduces verticality. It is less a ladder of promotions than a scaffold of interlocking skills. A copywriter who studies behavioural psychology doubles their value. A teacher who masters video editing monetises lessons online. A developer who adds public speaking transforms into a sought-after educator. Stacking multiplies worth across roles and revenue streams without starting anew each time.

This is not a call to become a polymath. It is about recognising transferable advantage. Three to five complementary skills often suffice. The power lies in synergy: a filmmaker fluent in distribution, a coach versed in digital marketing, a designer who can pitch, write, and deliver.

The chapter also dismantles the cultural myth equating hard work with progress. Effort alone, without strategic direction, can erode value. Many industrious individuals burn out in business models that cannot scale, trapped by loyalty to industries or income types that do not reward growth. The intellectual task, then, is to reframe productivity: measure not hours or tasks, but outcomes. Does current labour create assets or just invoices? Does it build transferable value or merely maintain deliverables?

This leads to asset-based thinking. One need not be a tech founder or property investor, but nearly anyone can craft activities that yield asymmetric returns—input decoupled from output over time. Writing a book, developing a newsletter, teaching a licensing course, producing templates, or creating a monetisable repository: these are forms of creative capital. They demand initial energy but generate future income independently of direct labour.

The barriers have diminished. Self-taught authors can reach international audiences. Subject-matter experts can engage thousands via accessible platforms. Developers can build a tool once and sell it repeatedly. Asset creation is no longer an elite preserve; it is increasingly a mindset.

Yet mindset alone is insufficient. Personal leverage identification—the process of locating one's unique intersection of skill, access, and advantage—is critical. Domain knowledge, technical fluency, charisma, or taste can all serve as levers. The goal is not imitation, but amplification of existing strengths.

Leverage often appears quietly: insight into systems, access to niche audiences, the ability to simplify complexity. Human leverage—reputation, networks, intellectual property—can rival financial leverage in potency, and it is widely accessible.

This chapter provides practical tools to identify, stack, and align these assets without reinventing identity or career. Whether a nurse exploring online education, a software engineer launching an info product, or an artist learning negotiation, the principles remain: structure efforts to compound, not merely accumulate. Think scaffolding, not sprinting.

Finally, the chapter interrogates the cultural fetishisation of busyness. Phrases like "I'm swamped" or "No rest for the ambitious" signal status but conceal stagnation. True financial progress is often quiet, deliberate, and spacious. It occurs through design, iteration, and deepening work—not constant motion. Redefining "enough" enables goals to be bigger yet better aligned. The ultimate flex is not the hundred-hour week, but sustainable autonomy, attention intact, engaging in meaningful work on terms you control.

Stacking income is not stacking tasks; it is stacking leverage. This chapter offers a blueprint to step off the treadmill and into a more intelligent, scalable relationship with earning—one that honours time, amplifies talent, and positions you not merely to survive, but to design.

The Skill Ladder, Not the Grind Loop-

The modern worker is exhausted, not just from the work itself, but from the fragmented psychology that underpins it. Endless productivity hacks, side gigs, and late-night hustles may feel proactive, but for many, they're quietly masking a more dangerous dynamic: stagnation disguised as motion. The grind loop—constantly scrambling for the next short-term income hit—is less a growth path and more a treadmill. And the longer one stays on it, the harder it becomes to see that there's another way entirely. That way is the *skill ladder*—a deliberate, compounding, and strategically vertical approach to building income through stacked, integrated capabilities rather than relentless task-chasing.

At its core, the grind loop is reactive. It incentivises urgency over depth, and fragmentation over focus. You freelance to fund today's needs, then freelance again tomorrow. You sell a product, only to rush into creating the next. It keeps the engine running, but not the plane flying higher. The skill ladder, by contrast, introduces a longer-term scaffolding to your earning power. Each skill acquired doesn't just add—it multiplies. And when combined intentionally, those skills start to generate asymmetric returns: more value, more trust, more leverage, and, crucially, more optionality.

Consider this contrast. A junior graphic designer who takes on ten low-cost client jobs a month may earn a functional income, but they're stuck in linear effort: income tied to time and delivery. Now imagine that same designer learns UX principles, then product strategy, then no-code development. Within 18 months, they've shifted from being hired to design what others envision, to co-creating interfaces, advising on customer experience, and even launching their own digital assets. Their value didn't double—it multiplied across domains. *This is income stacking through skill layering—not a new job, but a new economic identity.*

We often confuse skill with output, but true skill development builds *economic mobility*. That mobility comes not from collecting certificates, but from developing rare combinations. Two common misunderstandings block people from escaping the grind loop. First: the belief that mastering one skill is enough to future-proof you. Second: the belief that stacking skills means becoming a generalist. The truth lies in *intentional intersectionality*. Think of the copywriter who learns funnel strategy and suddenly commands five times the project rate. Or the software developer who understands sales psychology and is now building scalable SaaS tools with viral adoption. These are not random add-ons—they're stacked leverage.

And leverage is the operative word. Hustling harder increases output. Building layered skills increases *returns on output.* The more multidimensional your ability to solve high-value problems, the less you rely on volume. You start solving for *impact*, not effort. A videographer who understands narrative arcs and emotional pacing creates videos that convert. A marketer who can code small scripts to automate campaign workflows saves companies tens of thousands. These are not glamorous skills in themselves. But when strategically stacked, they create exponential differentiation.

This brings us to an uncomfortable truth: the culture of hustle, despite its seductive surface, is built on a scarcity model. Scarcity of time, of opportunity, of worth. It encourages you to monetise every waking hour, to commodify your attention, and to trade future creativity for present urgency. Skill stacking, by contrast, is abundance-based. It trains you to build, to wait, to think. It shifts your focus from *what can I earn this week?* to *what kind of economic leverage am I building this quarter, this year, this cycle?*

And yet, developing this mindset doesn't require quitting your job or becoming a founder overnight. It begins with a reframing: stop asking what's profitable *now*, and start asking what's *compoundable.* Skills that compound tend to meet three criteria: they apply across domains (transferability), they deepen with use (fluidity), and they unlock new categories of value (multiplication). Writing, storytelling, sales, technical literacy, negotiation, data fluency—none of these are new. But when built atop one another, they become rare capital. A data analyst who can explain findings to an executive audience is no longer just a number cruncher—they become a strategic bridge.

Importantly, the skill ladder is not a vertical hierarchy of status, but a lattice of value. Lateral moves matter. Often, the most valuable stacking happens not by advancing within a silo, but by moving across silos. A project manager who studies behavioural psychology doesn't just schedule more efficiently—they design better teams. A nurse who studies instructional design can teach, scale, and monetise what they know. The ladder is not about leaving your craft—it's about deepening your economic relevance through intelligent adjacency.

Critics of this model often raise concerns about time: "Where will I find space to learn new skills if I'm already stretched thin?" But this question reveals a deeper issue: *confusing busyness with traction.* Most grind loop behaviours are low-leverage by design. Spending 15 hours a week building a scalable skill or product—even slowly—is often more economically potent than 40 hours spent reacting to requests or chasing marginal gigs. The question, then, is not time *availability*—it's time *allocation.* What if the margin between surviving and thriving isn't 20 extra hours a week, but 10 smarter ones?

Another resistance point is the fear of abandoning identity. "But I'm a designer," or "I'm a writer." These labels are useful early on, but dangerous if left unexamined. The economy rewards those who build value, not those who guard titles. When you stack your design with behavioural economics, or your writing with analytics, or your engineering with storytelling, you don't lose identity—you expand it. Your personal brand stops being what you do and starts becoming *what you're capable of creating.*

Let's ground this with a real-world example. Consider the rise of creators who have become educators, operators who have become content producers, or consultants who have become product builders. The pattern is the same: *skill elasticity.* They didn't start with a master plan. They started with one deep skill, then paid attention to the adjacent gaps around them. The creator noticed people asking for tools. The consultant spotted recurring advice and turned it into IP. The educator saw how technology could scale their impact. These are not accidents—they are *patterns of intentional stacking.*

To begin this shift yourself, don't start with what you lack. Start with what you've already mastered—and map out its nearest neighbours. What does your current skill naturally complement? Where are you hitting ceilings, not because of lack of talent, but because of context? Where is the bottleneck—technical, persuasive, analytical, operational—that, if removed, would elevate your value immediately?

As you move through the rest of this chapter, you'll be given concrete frameworks to identify, prioritise, and combine skills in ways that make your income more resilient and your work more rewarding. But let this first principle anchor everything that follows: *income that multiplies is rarely the result of hustle alone. It's the product of deliberate design—through layered skills, applied intelligently over time.* And once you stop measuring productivity by exhaustion, and start measuring it by strategic leverage, your entire relationship with money—and work—begins to shift.

From Time-for-Money to Asset-Building

The most quietly destructive myth in modern personal finance is that working harder always leads to earning more. For generations, income has been framed as a direct trade-off: hours for money. The logic is deceptively simple—if you want to earn more, work more. But this exchange has a ceiling, and many hit it without even realising. There are only so many hours in a week, and each one has diminishing returns. The more significant cost, however, is opportunity: time spent earning money linearly is time not spent creating assets that could generate income while you sleep.

Asset-building is not the preserve of tech entrepreneurs or trust fund beneficiaries. It's a discipline available to any worker—creative, analytical, manual, or academic—who understands the leverage embedded in scalable effort. The shift begins with one foundational insight: *you don't get rich by what you earn; you get rich by what you own.* And what you own doesn't have to be physical. It can be intellectual property, systems, content, relationships, or licensing rights—intangible assets that outlast and outscale your own labour.

The difference between income and assets is more than just technical. It's psychological. Earning money through labour keeps the mind focused on immediate tasks, obligations, and deadlines. Building assets forces a longer view—decisions made today for payoffs tomorrow. It requires patience, abstraction, and trust in delayed gratification. But it is precisely this longer time horizon that opens the door to financial sovereignty.

One reason people remain trapped in labour-based income is because asset-building often doesn't "feel" productive at first. Writing a book draft, designing a course, coding a tool, or developing a licensing framework can take weeks, even months, before yielding revenue. Meanwhile, taking on another shift or client offers instant payment and psychological reward. Yet this short-term validation conceals the larger trap: *you are paid once for your time, but an asset pays you repeatedly for time you already spent.* That fundamental asymmetry is where freedom is won or lost.

Consider the distinction between a freelance graphic designer and a designer who sells templates or licenses work through a digital marketplace. The former earns linearly: they're paid per project, and every new client resets the clock. The latter earns exponentially: they create once and distribute endlessly, often earning from clients they've never met, across time zones they'll never visit. The shift from project-based income to product-based income is not merely tactical—it's strategic. It separates your earning potential from your personal bandwidth.

This principle extends across professions. A teacher who runs a tutoring business is bound by time. A teacher who develops a digital curriculum and licenses it to schools multiplies their effort. A fitness coach who trains clients one-on-one has a finite schedule. A coach who builds a digital membership platform has infinite scale. An attorney who charges by the hour earns based on scarcity. An attorney who packages legal templates or creates a subscription-based legal guidance system earns based on abundance. *The goal is not to work more efficiently, but to work categorically differently.*

It's worth addressing a common objection: "But I'm not technical." This concern is understandable, yet largely outdated. Asset-building in today's economy doesn't require coding or advanced tech fluency. Platforms like Gumroad, Teachable, Canva, Shopify, Substack, and Notion have dramatically lowered the barrier to entry. The key skill isn't programming—it's problem-solving. If you can solve a problem once, document it clearly, and package it thoughtfully, you can create an asset. Whether it's a digital guide, a niche service process, a planning tool, or a licensing model, the technology exists to turn personal expertise into income-generating assets.

The deeper challenge is not technical—it's conceptual. Asset-building requires shifting identity: from someone who *does work* to someone who *creates value.* That transition can be uncomfortable. It demands creative risk, the humility to iterate, and a willingness to endure dry spells before traction arrives. This is especially difficult in cultures that reward visible busyness and equate constant activity with ambition. *But financial independence is not earned through motion—it's earned through momentum, and momentum requires leverage.*

Another misconception is that asset-building must be large, flashy, or public. In reality, some of the most effective assets are small, quiet systems that solve specific problems for niche audiences. A Google Sheet that automates complex calculations. A PDF that helps freelancers set rates. A niche newsletter with affiliate links. A well-built backend for managing client leads. These assets are not glamorous, but they compound. And more importantly, they decouple income from daily effort.

The most sustainable approach to asset-building is incremental. Begin by asking: "What have I built or solved repeatedly for others that could be documented or packaged?" Then, test the smallest viable version. Launch it quietly. Refine based on real user input. Avoid perfectionism; your first asset doesn't need to be a bestseller. It just needs to exist. What matters is that it shifts the dynamic—you are no longer purely a worker, but a builder. *That identity shift is the seed of financial autonomy.*

Time-based income builds security. Asset-based income builds resilience. It gives you optionality. When your rent is covered by a product you built six months ago, your entire posture toward work changes. You negotiate differently. You take strategic risks. You walk away from toxic clients. You say no more often. *Assets don't just increase income—they increase agency.*

For self-employed readers, asset-building can create a buffer during off seasons or client droughts. For employees, assets offer a parallel path—side income that doesn't require burning out through side gigs. For anyone, they offer a kind of career antifragility: the ability to generate value without constant personal exertion. This is especially critical in an economic landscape increasingly shaped by automation, volatility, and remote work. The more your income depends on your direct time, the more vulnerable you are. The more it depends on assets, the more protected—and empowered—you become.

Asset-building is not a replacement for skill-building. It is a *byproduct* of it. The most effective assets emerge from layered expertise—knowledge that has been earned, tested, and refined. This is where the idea of "income stacking" meets its full expression. Each skill you acquire—copywriting, photography, negotiation, systems thinking, public speaking—doesn't just add value; it multiplies when paired with a complementary skill. You move from being a one-dimensional expert to a multidimensional problem-solver. And when those layers are expressed through assets, you're no longer trading time for money—you're trading *insight for leverage.*

To be clear, not every asset will succeed. Some will underperform. Others will fail outright. But even the failures are investments. They teach, they clarify, they evolve. More importantly, they condition your brain to think in terms of systems and scale. That cognitive shift alone is worth the effort. Once you learn to spot reusable value, you stop seeing your workday as a to-do list and start seeing it as a portfolio. You stop optimising for efficiency and start optimising for leverage. That change is what separates earners from builders—and employees from architects.

The promise of asset-building is not overnight success. It's durable success. Income that flows even when you pause. Opportunities that arise without chasing. A financial life designed around autonomy, not exhaustion. The question is not whether you have the time to build assets. The real question is: *can you afford not to?*

Finding Your Leverage Point-

Most people vastly underestimate the value of what they already have—and overestimate the need to start from scratch. In a culture obsessed with hustle and reinvention, we rarely pause to examine what's already working in our favour. But in reality, the people who build disproportionate wealth are rarely the most talented, the hardest working, or the most visible. They are the ones who find and compound *leverage*—those subtle, often hidden advantages that let them do more with less, reach further with fewer steps, and earn bigger returns from smaller moves.

Leverage is not luck. It's clarity. And once identified, it can be engineered, cultivated, and scaled. Yet most people remain blind to it, not because they lack intelligence, but because they've been conditioned to see their efforts only in terms of volume: more effort equals more reward. But modern economic mobility is not about effort. It's about direction and advantage. Two people can work the same number of hours, yet produce wildly different outcomes—because one is using leverage and the other is trading effort for marginal gain.

Leverage comes in many forms: specialised skills, unique combinations of knowledge, strategic positioning, credibility in a niche, cultural fluency, a reputation for integrity, a highly curated network, or even a deep understanding of timing in a particular market. *Unfair advantages are rarely dramatic; they're usually cumulative.* Someone who has been writing publicly for three years may not be more intelligent than you—but they've built trust, distribution, and momentum. Someone with industry-specific vocabulary and client context may win deals not because they are better, but because they are familiar. Recognition, in almost every domain, is a function of resonance—and resonance is leverage.

The first task is not to chase leverage. It's to recognise what leverage you already have but haven't named. Begin by examining where others consistently come to you for advice or help. Patterns are rarely accidents. If multiple people seek your guidance on hiring, editing, positioning, or decision-making, it's not anecdotal—it's a signal. Often we discount what comes easily to us, assuming that it must be easy for everyone. But ease is not irrelevance; *ease is often mastery in disguise.*

It's also worth reflecting on your overlaps—the intersections where your skills or experiences converge in unique ways. A software engineer who understands storytelling. A therapist with sales expertise. A musician with business acumen. These combinations are often more valuable than deep expertise in a single domain. *The rarest leverage comes not from depth alone, but from the synthesis of unrelated competencies.* Hybrid knowledge creates asymmetric advantage, especially in markets hungry for context-specific insights.

The second tier of leverage is network-based. Not the generic "your network is your net worth" sentiment, but the sober reality that introductions, endorsements, and proximity often outperform credentials. In a world of infinite information, *people filter through trust.* If someone trusted introduces your work, it carries more weight than any ad spend or cold email could. This is why thoughtful relationship-building—grounded in reciprocity, not extraction—is a form of capital. It compounds in unpredictable but powerful ways.

But leverage is not only additive. It is often subtractive. It's the ability to say no to non-leveraged activities. It's the clarity to ignore prestige in favour of control. It's knowing when to step back from clients, gigs, or roles that cap your growth ceiling. *You cannot find your leverage point if your time is fragmented by obligations that dilute your focus.* Saying no is a skill not of defiance, but of design. Every yes that isn't strategic is a no to compounding leverage elsewhere.

An important truth here is that leverage is not always visible to you—but it is often obvious to others. This is where feedback becomes crucial. Ask a few people who know your work well: "What do you think I do better than most?" or "Where do you think I've created outsized value with less effort?" Their answers may point you to leverage you've normalised. This is not about false humility or shallow praise. It's about surfacing blind spots. We're often the last to see our own momentum, because we're buried inside it.

Once identified, leverage must be *designed for.* This is where most people falter. They assume leverage is static—something to be found and left alone. But real leverage compounds only when built into systems. If your unique advantage is clarity under pressure, how do you package that into consulting frameworks or decision tools? If your edge is an insider network in a growing industry, how do you transform that into deal flow, curated content, or advisory opportunities? If you're unusually good at simplifying complexity, how do you translate that into writing, products, or speaking engagements? *Leverage must be channelled to be useful. Otherwise, it dissipates as background competency.*

This design phase often involves narrowing your audience—not broadening it. Mass-market appeal is rarely a leverage strategy. It forces you to compete with louder, cheaper, or more resourced players. Specificity, by contrast, increases magnetism. Being known as "the person who helps early-stage founders de-risk hiring" is infinitely more powerful than being "a business consultant." Leverage grows in niches. From there, it radiates outward.

Crucially, finding leverage doesn't mean abandoning fundamentals. Grit, learning, and resilience matter. But those qualities are force multipliers, not substitutes. It is better to be moderately skilled but well-leveraged than to be brilliant but misapplied. Many intelligent, capable people remain undercompensated and overwhelmed—not because they lack ability, but because they have never asked the harder, more important question: *What can I do that scales beyond my own input?*

That question leads to positioning. Strategic positioning is a form of invisible leverage. It's not what you do—it's how others frame what you do. A graphic designer positioned as a "brand systems advisor" will command more trust and revenue than one who is seen as a commodity. A content writer who is known for "converting expertise into thought leadership" will earn more than one simply labelled "freelance writer." Positioning creates leverage because it affects how your work is priced, perceived, and prioritised. *How you are seen determines what you are paid for—even more than what you deliver.*

There's also the question of timing. Not all leverage is permanent. Sometimes, it's circumstantial: a cultural trend you understand early, a tool you've mastered before the market catches up, a geography or language edge that puts you closer to an emerging opportunity. Timing-based leverage is fleeting but potent. Recognising it requires peripheral awareness: scanning beyond your bubble, asking contrarian questions, and moving before certainty arrives. This is not gambling—it's informed risk-taking, backed by pattern recognition.

Of course, leverage also comes with responsibility. Used carelessly, it becomes exploitation. But when wielded with integrity, it creates win-wins: you serve more people at scale while reducing your own burnout. You create options, not obligations. You build income streams, not just to-do lists. You turn your strengths into scaffolding—not just for career growth, but for impact, autonomy, and long-term resilience.

Ultimately, leverage is not something you wait to earn—it's something you choose to locate. Not through force, but through pattern recognition. Not through grind, but through reflection. The most successful professionals are not simply talented or tireless. They're leveraged. They've identified where their inputs create exponential outputs—and they've had the discipline to double down.

If you're constantly exhausted and underpaid, the issue may not be your effort or ethics. It may simply be that you're applying force where you should be applying *leverage.*

Rejecting the Busy Myth-

Somewhere along the line, "busy" became a badge of honour. We use it as a default answer, a social signal, even a subtle form of self-justification. But beneath the surface of constant activity lies a sobering question: *busy doing what, exactly—and to what end?* The conflation of motion with progress has quietly distorted how we measure value, productivity, and success. Especially in the financial domain, busyness has become a proxy for ambition, when in reality it often camouflages avoidance, inefficiency, and unexamined insecurity.

The economics of modern work no longer reward sheer volume. They reward *clarity, leverage, and decision-making under complexity.* Yet most people remain trapped in what can be described as the "effort economy"—where the perceived worth of work is tethered to the visible strain of doing it. This is especially pervasive among high-achieving professionals, self-employed creatives, and early-career builders, for whom exhaustion often masquerades as evidence of progress. But productivity should not be confused with depletion. The obsession with busyness isn't a neutral cultural quirk. It's a costly psychological trap.

The busyness myth thrives because it feels emotionally safer than strategic stillness. Constant doing inoculates us against the discomfort of confronting misalignment. It delays the deeper work of defining enough. And it feeds a fragile identity—one built not on outcomes or contribution, but on *effort signalling*. In this frame, taking a break feels indulgent, boundaries feel lazy, and stillness becomes suspect. But if your financial life is built on proving you're hardworking rather than producing actual strategic results, the system is already broken.

Real financial productivity is quiet. It happens in well-structured systems, not frantic improvisation. It prioritises consistency over adrenaline. It requires the maturity to differentiate between doing *many* things and doing *the right* things. Financial traction isn't about how many hours you've spent inside a spreadsheet or how many side gigs you're juggling. It's about how well your efforts compound. And compounding, by definition, demands patience, design, and focus—not perpetual hustle.

The most dangerous thing about chronic busyness is that it robs you of perspective. When every spare moment is consumed with output, there's no cognitive space left for reflection, recalibration, or strategic reallocation. You become the operator of your financial life—but never its architect. You respond rather than design. And in doing so, you risk building a future optimised for *activity*, not *autonomy*.

The mythology of hustle has its roots in a scarcity mindset: the idea that unless you are constantly proving your worth through motion, someone else will surpass you. But that logic collapses under scrutiny. True economic security is not earned through perpetual grind. It is earned through systems that work *even when you're not*. Passive income, asset-backed income, process-driven consulting, productised services, and strategic licensing—these are not theoretical ideals; they are evidence that financial productivity can and must be decoupled from constant activity.

There is also a gendered and racialised layer to this myth. For many, being "seen to be busy" is not just performative—it's protective. In environments where credibility is earned under biased scrutiny, busyness becomes a way of pre-empting judgment. But this too carries a cost: it enforces a loop of overwork that ultimately erodes clarity, confidence, and long-term health. To reject the busy myth is not to reject effort—it is to reject performative depletion as a metric of worth.

A healthy financial life is defined by *effectiveness, not effort.* You don't get paid for being busy. You get paid for creating value that matters, in ways that scale, repeat, and align with your long-term goals. That might mean spending 30 focused minutes restructuring a retainer agreement that improves cash flow for a year. Or deciding *not* to accept one more short-term client if it derails your long-term product roadmap. Or automating a savings plan so that willpower and spreadsheets are no longer daily friction points. *Less drama, more results.*

The question, then, is not how to do more—it's how to define what *enough* means in your financial context. This definition is not a limitation; it's a liberation. Without a clear concept of enough, you will default to infinite pursuit. You will chase more clients, more revenue, more visibility, without ever converting those inputs into actual stability or satisfaction. But *enough is not a number. It is a design choice.* It's the threshold at which your money serves your life, not consumes it. It's where your systems take over from your adrenaline. It's where growth becomes sustainable, not compulsive.

This redefinition has profound implications. When you define enough, you reclaim autonomy over your time, attention, and energy. You stop trading your evenings for marginal revenue. You stop saying yes to unstrategic work. You stop mistaking responsiveness for relevance. And you begin to optimise for your *real priorities*—be that creative focus, family presence, geographic mobility, or simply peace of mind.

But to do this well, you must also resist the ambient pressure to keep up. Busyness has become a cultural currency, and opting out will often invite critique—from peers, clients, even your own inner critic.

"Are you doing enough?" becomes a whispered refrain. That's when it's critical to remember: *a calendar full of motion is not evidence of progress.* You don't owe anyone the performance of effort. You owe yourself a financial life that works in practice, not just in performance.

There is, of course, a difference between seasonal hustle and chronic busyness. In moments of strategic expansion, intense effort is often required. But that effort should serve a specific design—not become a lifestyle default. Temporary sprints are valuable; perpetual sprinting is unsustainable. Every system has a load-bearing limit. Your nervous system is no exception.

A practical exercise: audit your financial calendar—not in terms of tasks, but in terms of *return on clarity, cash flow, and strategic direction.* Which activities moved the needle? Which were driven by fear, people-pleasing, or compulsive busyness? What can be delegated, automated, or eliminated entirely? Where are you substituting volume for impact? The answers won't just improve your time management; they'll transform your financial trajectory.

Ultimately, the choice to reject the busy myth is not about doing less. It's about *doing deliberately.* It's about recognising that a meaningful financial life cannot be built on a foundation of frantic motion. It requires space to think, time to design, and the courage to say no to what is merely urgent so you can build what is truly important. Because if you don't define what enough looks like, someone else will define it for you—and it will always be *more.*

When you stop chasing busyness, you make room for *strategy.* When you stop equating value with effort, you start building systems that compound. And when you define enough, you finally begin to live—not just work. That, in the end, is real financial productivity: *not how much you do, but how aligned your money is with your actual values.*

Chapter 7
Your First Investments

The veneration of the hustle has become almost instinctive—a cultural reflex equating exhaustion with virtue and ceaseless busyness with ambition. It permeates side gigs, the aesthetics of grind culture, and the widespread belief that longer hours automatically yield financial freedom. Yet beneath the surface, many racing toward the next invoice, freelance client, or gig are really on a treadmill rather than a track: the calendar fills, the scenery changes, but their financial altitude barely shifts. This chapter offers a different approach: not how to hustle harder, but how to stack smarter.

Earning power is rarely a simple function of effort; it is magnified through design. Those who are financially stable and creatively fulfilled do not necessarily work the longest hours. They've learned to stack skills into leverage. They identify capabilities that compound—writing, design, strategy, coding, negotiation, communication—and arrange them to expand value across markets and contexts. They move beyond selling time to building systems, assets, or ideas that generate returns without linear labour. This is income stacking: cultivating layered competencies to create optionality, scalability, and durability.

Consider two freelancers. One dedicates forty hours a week chasing clients, billing hourly, delivering bespoke work from scratch each cycle. The other structures a skill-based ecosystem: consulting three days a week, licensing a course or template, running a newsletter with affiliate income, and managing a quarterly cohort programme. The first works harder; the second earns more. The difference is not hustle—it is design.

Design begins by escaping the grind loop: a behavioural trap where motion masquerades as progress. The loop is seductive, flattering the ego with activity while quietly draining strategic attention. Exhausted, you default to what feels immediately productive, and earning potential plateaus—not from lack of effort, but from lack of elevation.

Income stacking introduces verticality. Think less of a ladder of promotions and more of a scaffold of interlocking skills. A copywriter who studies behavioural psychology can double their value. A teacher who learns video editing monetises lessons online. A developer who adds public speaking becomes a sought-after educator. Stacking multiplies worth across roles, industries, and income streams without starting from zero each time.

This is not a call to become a polymath. It is a framework for recognising transferable advantage. You do not need ten unrelated skills—three to five complementary ones suffice. The power lies in interaction: a filmmaker who understands distribution, a coach fluent in digital marketing, a designer who can pitch, write, and deliver.

The chapter also deconstructs the cultural myth equating hard work with progress. Effort alone, without direction, can erode value. Millions of diligent individuals burn out in business models that cannot scale, trapped by loyalty to industries or income types that fail to reward growth. The intellectual task is to reframe productivity: measure not hours or output, but outcomes. Does your labour create assets or merely invoices? Does it build transferable value or maintain deliverables?

This shifts the focus from time-for-money to asset-based thinking. Few need to become tech founders or property investors, but nearly everyone can cultivate activities that generate asymmetric returns—inputs decoupled from outputs over time. Writing a book, building a newsletter audience, teaching a licensing course, crafting a visual template, or producing a monetisable podcast: these are forms of creative capital. They demand upfront effort but yield ongoing income without continuous input.

For sceptics, it may sound improbable. Yet barriers have fallen. A self-taught author can reach international audiences. A subject-matter expert can teach thousands via free platforms. A coder can create a small tool once and sell it repeatedly. Asset-building is no longer elite—it is increasingly a mindset.

Mindset alone is insufficient. Personal leverage identification—the process of locating one's unique intersection of skill, access, and advantage—is crucial. Some have domain knowledge, others charisma, technical fluency, or taste. The goal is not replication but amplification of existing strengths.

Leverage can be quiet: understanding a system, access to a niche audience, the ability to simplify complexity. Human leverage—reputation, networks, intellectual property—can rival financial leverage in power, and it is widely accessible.

This chapter provides practical tools to identify, stack, and align these assets without reinventing identity or career. Whether a nurse exploring online education, a software engineer creating an info product, or an artist learning negotiation, the principles remain: structure income-building efforts to compound, not just accumulate. Think scaffolding, not sprinting.

Finally, we interrogate the cultural obsession with busyness. Phrases like "I'm swamped" or "No rest for the ambitious" signal status but conceal stagnation. True financial progress is often quiet and deliberate. It emerges through design, iteration, and deepening work—not constant motion. Redefining "enough" ensures goals are not only larger but aligned. The ultimate measure of success is not a hundred-hour week, but sustainable autonomy: attention intact, doing work that matters, on terms you define.

Stacking income is not about stacking tasks. It is about stacking leverage. This chapter offers a blueprint to step off the treadmill and cultivate a more intelligent, scalable relationship with earning—one that respects time, amplifies talent, and positions you not merely to survive, but to design.

Why Saving Alone Won't Cut It-

The idea that consistent saving is the bedrock of financial security has been passed down with near-religious conviction: live beneath your means, squirrel away a portion of each paycheque, and eventually, you'll be rewarded with peace of mind. But this well-worn advice, while not wrong in spirit, is dangerously incomplete in substance. In today's economic reality—where inflation quietly drains the value of idle money, where technological disruption reshapes industries overnight, and where longevity pushes retirement horizons into our 70s—saving alone is not enough. It's a start, but it is no longer a strategy.

To understand why, we must begin with a simple, unsettling truth: *money loses value over time.* Inflation is not a theoretical concept—it's a real, compounding erosion of purchasing power. A pound saved today does not hold its full weight a decade from now. Even modest inflation, say 2.5% annually, reduces the real value of your savings by nearly 22% over 10 years. For savers relying on bank accounts with near-zero interest, that erosion is effectively guaranteed. It's not visible like a market drop, but its long-term effects are just as damaging. Saving, in such a context, can feel responsible but still lead to stagnation.

But inflation is only part of the equation. The greater threat to wealth-building is *opportunity cost*—the quiet forfeiture of what your money could have earned had it been working elsewhere. While savings accounts preserve nominal value, investments grow real value. Consider this: £10,000 sitting in a standard bank account for 20 years might grow to £12,000 with interest. The same amount invested in a low-cost index fund, assuming a conservative average return of 7% per annum, becomes nearly £40,000 over the same period. The gap isn't marginal—it's exponential. What's being missed is not just interest, but compounded growth: the ability of money to generate more money simply by staying invested.

Time, therefore, is not just a factor—it's the force multiplier. The earlier you invest, the less you need to save later. This isn't motivational fluff; it's hard arithmetic. A 25-year-old who invests £200 per month at 7% annual growth will likely surpass the total wealth of a 40-year-old who starts investing twice that amount. The difference isn't income, discipline, or intelligence—it's *start date*. Time in the market consistently beats timing the market. Yet the myth that one must be "ready" or "wealthy enough" to start investing keeps millions on the sidelines, unknowingly giving up their most powerful advantage.

The hesitation often stems from fear—a sense that investing is inherently risky or too complex. But the greater risk is misunderstanding what "safe" really means. Savings accounts are safe from volatility but not from decay. They are safe in the short term but ineffective in the long run. By contrast, diversified investing—especially in broad, low-cost equity indices—has historically proven one of the most resilient engines for wealth accumulation. The key is not avoiding risk, but learning to manage it in line with your goals, time horizon, and tolerance.

Part of the problem lies in how we conceptualise financial security. Saving is framed as an act of prudence, while investing is often framed as speculation. This cultural framing reinforces inaction. But investing is not gambling when done responsibly. It is, at its best, a way of aligning your financial actions with long-term autonomy. It's about building systems that continue to grow while you sleep, work, rest, or navigate life's uncertainties. It's about *multiplication*, not just accumulation.

Moreover, we must challenge the belief that income alone will carry us across the finish line. Even a high salary, if entirely consumed or hoarded in cash, offers no path to scalable wealth. Without investment, income is a treadmill: the pace might vary, but the motion is circular. Wealth, by contrast, is about escape velocity—the moment when your assets begin to generate enough returns to reduce your dependence on labour. That freedom isn't reserved for the elite; it begins with the decision to make your money *work* alongside you.

To be clear, saving still has its place. Emergency funds, short-term goals, and buffers for uncertainty are all essential. But these are foundations, not destinations. Treating savings as the endpoint of financial responsibility is akin to stopping at the runway and never taking flight. Investing is what lifts your financial life into future-oriented motion. It's the act of transforming money from a static resource into a dynamic tool.

This transition from saver to investor also requires a mindset shift. Many people assume they need expertise, luck, or constant vigilance to succeed. But most wealth is not built by clever stock picking—it's built by disciplined, automated participation in growth markets. Tools like index funds, target-date funds, and robo-advisors have democratised access to markets without requiring expert knowledge. What's needed is not brilliance, but *consistency*.

Let's consider a real-world illustration. Imagine two professionals: both earn £50,000 per year, and both manage to save £5,000 annually. One keeps the entire amount in a high-interest savings account earning 1%. The other invests in a diversified portfolio averaging 6%. After 15 years, the saver has around £87,000. The investor has over £130,000. They saved the same amount—but only one allowed their money to grow *beyond their labour*. Over time, that divergence accelerates. It's not about working harder. It's about positioning money to do some of the work for you.

This is where time, psychology, and economics converge. Because the person who invests builds not only a portfolio, but also a sense of agency. They begin to see money not as something to guard, but as something to *deploy*. They understand that wealth isn't about hoarding, but about positioning capital in ways that align with the life they want. Investing, at its core, is a statement: I trust the future enough to prepare for it.

To reject investing is not to opt out of risk—it is to guarantee a different kind of risk: falling behind. As wages stagnate and costs rise, even diligent savers may find their efforts insufficient. What once looked like prudence begins to look like self-imposed scarcity. The pathway out of this is not speculation, but *structure*. It's about creating a long-term plan for your money that involves risk-adjusted growth, diversified exposure, and intentional compounding. You don't need to be perfect. You just need to participate.

Equally important is redefining what success looks like. Investing isn't about beating the market or turning into a financial guru. It's about expanding your options. It's about knowing that if you want to change jobs, take a sabbatical, start a business, or support someone you love, you won't be wholly dependent on your next paycheque. Investing is not a trophy—it's a tool. And it is one that can be shaped to reflect your values, goals, and life design.

So if you've been diligently saving, that's commendable. But now it's time to go further. Saving is the discipline. Investing is the leverage. Saving keeps you afloat. Investing moves you forward. The sooner that shift happens, the more control you gain—not just over your money, but over your time, choices, and future self.

Understanding this isn't just an economic insight—it's a behavioural commitment. It means learning the vocabulary, confronting the discomfort, and building a system that allows you to act before you feel fully ready. Because no one feels completely ready. The difference is that investors move anyway. They begin small. They build habits. And over time, those habits create momentum that savings alone cannot deliver.

Let the next pound you save not just sit, but *grow*. Let it be the first brick in a structure that supports the life you want—not someday, but step by step. Because saving might protect you, but only investing can truly *free* you.

Learning to Speak the Language-

Most people enter the world of investing not with confidence, but with caution, often shadowed by the feeling that everyone else understands something they don't. The acronyms are opaque. The jargon feels deliberately alienating. Terms like "equities," "dividends," "capital gains," or "index tracking" sound either intimidating or indistinguishable, depending on prior exposure. But finance is not a native tongue—it's a learned language. And like any language, it can be mastered not by memorising definitions, but by internalising concepts in context. To build wealth intelligently, one doesn't need an economics degree or insider credentials; one needs fluency. And fluency begins with understanding—not shortcuts, not tips, but depth.

The reason financial language feels exclusionary is not accidental. For decades, much of the investment world thrived on opacity. Complexity was equated with legitimacy. If you didn't understand it, you were told to trust the professionals who did. But modern investing—particularly for individuals building autonomy, not empires—requires *clarity*, not complexity. It requires that we take hold of the language used to describe money, risk, growth, and decision-making, so that we're not just passive consumers of financial advice but active stewards of our capital.

At the core of financial fluency is the ability to distinguish between *risk* and *volatility*. They're often used interchangeably, but they refer to different things. Volatility is the degree to which an asset's price fluctuates over time—it's emotional, visible, and can be unsettling. Risk, by contrast, is the probability of losing money permanently. A volatile asset may drop and recover. A risky asset may collapse and never return. Equating the two can lead to flawed decisions, like selling a sound investment during a downturn or avoiding productive markets entirely. Fluency means knowing that volatility is not a verdict, but a feature of markets—something to be understood, not feared.

Likewise, the concept of *diversification* often gets reduced to a buzzword, but its power lies in nuance. True diversification isn't just holding a mix of stocks and bonds; it's about holding *uncorrelated* assets—investments that respond differently to the same economic event. A portfolio with 20 different tech stocks isn't diversified; it's crowded. A portfolio that includes domestic equities, international exposure, real estate, and bonds, even in modest amounts, is far more resilient. Fluency here means grasping the function of an asset class, not just its label.

Another foundational term is *compound interest*—the exponential growth that occurs when earnings themselves begin to earn. The mechanics are simple, but the implications are profound. Someone who starts investing at 25 and contributes steadily will almost always outperform someone who starts at 40, even if the latter saves more annually. Compound growth rewards time more than effort, patience more than perfection. Understanding this isn't just math—it's mindset. It shifts focus from urgent returns to sustained participation.

Moving from principles to instruments, it's vital to distinguish between *active* and *passive* investing. Active investing involves selecting individual stocks or timing the market, usually with the aim of outperforming an index. It's labour-intensive, emotionally charged, and rarely successful over long periods—especially after fees. Passive investing, by contrast, tracks the market through instruments like index funds or ETFs. It is cost-effective, systematic, and supported by decades of empirical evidence. Fluency doesn't mean you must choose one over the other, but that you understand what each method implies in terms of risk, effort, and expected outcome.

Terms like *ETF* (Exchange-Traded Fund), *mutual fund*, or *REIT* (Real Estate Investment Trust) are often misunderstood. An ETF is a basket of securities—like a mutual fund—that trades like a stock. It offers diversification, liquidity, and typically low fees. A mutual fund may be actively or passively managed, but usually incurs higher costs. A REIT allows you to invest in property without owning physical real estate, often yielding dividends but also susceptible to interest rate sensitivity. These aren't just products; they are tools. Understanding their structure and purpose allows you to select them not out of habit, but out of alignment with your strategy.

Fluency also includes recognising psychological terms that govern investor behaviour—*loss aversion*, *confirmation bias*, *herd behaviour*. These cognitive biases affect even experienced investors. Loss aversion, for example, describes how the pain of losing money often outweighs the pleasure of gaining it. This can lead to holding on to bad investments too long or exiting good ones too soon. To be financially literate is not only to speak the language of markets but to understand the language of your own mind within them.

Then there are the regulatory distinctions. Knowing what an *ISA* (Individual Savings Account) is in the UK, and how it differs from a *pension* (such as a SIPP—Self-Invested Personal Pension), can determine tax efficiency. An ISA allows you to invest up to a certain annual limit without paying capital gains or income tax. A pension gives tax relief on contributions but locks up the money until a certain age. Understanding these distinctions enables you to *optimise* your wealth strategy—not just accumulate capital, but retain more of it.

Importantly, investment language also includes macroeconomic concepts that shape market behaviour: *interest rates*, *inflation*, *monetary policy*, *fiscal stimulus*. These forces do not require daily tracking, but ignoring them entirely is like sailing without understanding wind. When interest rates rise, for example, borrowing becomes more expensive, which can affect business profits, consumer spending, and therefore stock valuations. When inflation accelerates, cash loses value faster—making growth-oriented investments more urgent. Financial fluency means interpreting headlines not as noise, but as context for smart decisions.

To be fluent does not mean to be encyclopaedic. It means that when you hear "dividend yield," you know it reflects income relative to price. When someone discusses "market capitalisation," you understand it's the value of a company's shares in total, not an indicator of quality. It means you're not intimidated by terminology because you grasp the underlying mechanics. And most importantly, it means you're no longer a passive recipient of financial narratives—you're an active participant in shaping your own.

The shift from financial illiteracy to fluency is not a leap, but a progression. It happens through exposure, repetition, reflection, and application. It's reading a statement and asking what each figure represents. It's listening to a podcast and pausing to verify a term. It's noticing which words still make you uncomfortable, and refusing to let that discomfort breed avoidance. The market doesn't reward only those with knowledge—it rewards those who act on knowledge consistently.

We must also dismantle the myth that speaking the language of investing requires sacrificing clarity. On the contrary, clarity is fluency. If an advisor, article, or platform can't explain something in plain terms, the problem is not with your understanding—it's with their articulation. Financial literacy isn't about sounding smart; it's about making smart decisions. It's about equipping yourself with the vocabulary to ask sharper questions, to spot bad advice, and to understand *why* you're investing—not just *what* you're investing in.

There's a quiet empowerment that comes when you can read a financial document and not feel alienated. When you can decode a fund fact sheet, interpret risk levels, or compare fee structures without guessing. This empowerment doesn't come from shortcuts. It comes from engaging with the language repeatedly, deliberately, and with curiosity. And the reward is not just knowledge—it's agency.

Ultimately, learning to speak the language of investing is not a technical achievement—it's a foundational shift in identity. You move from being a consumer of financial products to a designer of financial outcomes. You stop outsourcing your autonomy and begin building it, word by word, concept by concept. And that fluency, once developed, compounds—just like your investments.

The Fear Equation-

Most people don't begin investing because they're confident. They begin because they're uneasy—about inflation, about job security, about not wanting to be the person who worked for 40 years and still worries about rent. But when it comes to actually putting money into markets, unease often doesn't translate into action. It curdles into avoidance. For many young people today, the idea of investing triggers a complex, paralysing emotion—a combination of fear, shame, uncertainty, and distrust. The hesitation is rarely about numbers. It's about risk and identity. It's about not wanting to look foolish. It's about a fear equation in which the perceived downside of doing something wrong outweighs the possible upside of doing something right.

This fear is not irrational. It's adaptive. Many young adults came of age during, or just after, the 2008 financial crisis—an event that revealed how rigged, opaque, and ruthless the financial system can be. The names may have changed—Enron became Lehman

Brothers, which became FTX—but the cultural memory remains: people who played by the rules lost homes, jobs, and retirement accounts. That backdrop fosters a deep scepticism, especially among those without familial wealth or guidance. The idea that markets are "safe in the long run" feels abstract, if not deliberately evasive.

Yet paradoxically, this fear—while emotionally valid—often becomes more costly than the risk itself. Because while doing nothing feels safe, it carries its own, invisible risk: the erosion of time. Inflation doesn't make noise. Opportunity cost doesn't send alerts. But they're happening, every day. A pound sitting in cash is losing value at 2–4% annually in real terms. Compound growth, the most powerful force in long-term wealth creation, is a function of time in the market—not timing it. *Waiting to feel ready is the most expensive investment strategy of all.*

So why is the fear equation so potent? Part of it is cultural. Western education systems, particularly in the UK and US, rarely teach financial fluency. That means for many, the first real exposure to investing comes through hearsay, YouTube personalities, or social media speculation. If you've never been taught the basics of diversification, fees, or index funds, then of course investing looks like gambling. The platforms are gamified. The influencers push exotic instruments. And without context, any loss—however small—feels like proof that this world isn't built for you.

But there's also a psychological dimension. Investing forces you to confront uncertainty. There are no guarantees. You are making a decision today that won't bear fruit for 5, 10, or 30 years. And that decision feels public—like you might "fail" in front of people. In that light, it makes sense why so many defer. The embarrassment of a perceived mistake feels more real than the abstract upside of delayed autonomy. This is the core of the fear equation: *the pain of loss is felt more intensely than the reward of gain.* Behavioural economists call this loss aversion. It's not a weakness; it's a bias. But left unexamined, it can shape entire lifetimes.

There's also a myth of perfection that underpins much of this paralysis. People want to invest "the right way"—the perfect fund, the ideal allocation, the correct entry point. But that belief presupposes a level of predictability that markets don't offer. In truth, most professional fund managers can't beat the market over long periods. The idea that a first-time investor will somehow find the perfect timing or product is not only unrealistic—it's unnecessary. *The most important decision is not precision; it's participation.* A globally diversified fund held over decades will outperform 99% of speculative bets. But to benefit, you must be in the game.

So how do we shift the fear equation? The answer lies in reframing. First, redefine what "loss" means. If you invest £500 and it drops to £450, that's not a failure—it's volatility. That number will change. What matters is your behaviour, not the market's. Did you panic and sell? Or did you trust your plan and hold? Long-term investors don't win because they predict markets; they win because they don't interrupt compounding. Your job is not to avoid dips—it's to survive them.

Second, adopt a systems mindset. If every investment decision requires emotional energy, you'll burn out or make poor choices. Instead, automate the process. Set up a monthly transfer into a low-cost index fund. Treat it like a bill—consistent, boring, and non-negotiable. Automation sidesteps the fear loop by removing decision points. You don't need to be brave every month. You only need to be brave once.

Third, lower the stakes. Start small. Not just financially, but psychologically. The goal of your first £100 investment is not to make money—it's to learn. To see how markets move. To watch your emotions respond. That learning is more valuable than any short-term return. Once investing becomes familiar, the fear diminishes—not because the risk disappears, but because *you've grown to accommodate it.*

It's also essential to interrogate your sources. Are your fears based on experience, or on headlines? Are you reacting to your own understanding, or someone else's drama? Financial media thrives on exaggeration. Sensationalism sells. But your portfolio is not a news cycle. One of the most underrated skills in investing is *selective attention*—knowing which noise to ignore, and which signals to act on. Most of the time, the best response to fear-inducing news is no action at all.

Mindset is not just motivational fluff—it's infrastructure. And one of the most liberating shifts a young investor can make is to stop viewing investing as an identity test. You are not your portfolio. It doesn't reflect your intelligence or worth. It is simply a tool—like a pen, or a passport. You don't need to be perfect with it. You just need to use it consistently, thoughtfully, and with enough humility to adjust when needed.

There's also value in understanding the emotional arc of investing. Every investor, whether managing £500 or £5 million, goes through fear. It's not a phase to outgrow, but a force to manage. What changes over time is not that fear disappears—but that *you stop letting it drive.* You begin to expect volatility. You understand that temporary dips are not terminal. You build systems that absorb emotional shocks. And you begin to trust, not in the market, but in your own capacity to stay the course.

Finally, there's the question of fraud and exploitation—a fear that's sadly grounded in reality. There are scams. There are bad actors. But avoiding all investing because some areas are risky is like avoiding all food because some items are contaminated. Instead, apply the same scepticism you use elsewhere. Check fees. Use regulated platforms. Prefer simplicity over opacity. If you can't explain the investment in one or two clear sentences, you probably don't understand it well enough to trust it.

Investing is not about erasing fear. It's about building a different relationship to it—one rooted in education, structure, and perspective. You begin by acknowledging the emotion, then designing habits that act independently of it. The best investors aren't fearless. They are simply disciplined. And discipline, unlike fearlessness, is something you can cultivate.

This reframing doesn't make risk disappear. But it makes it intelligible. And when risk becomes intelligible, it becomes manageable. The fear equation—once reframed—starts to yield a different result. Loss is no longer identity-threatening. Uncertainty is no longer paralysing. Markets become a context for growth, not a source of dread.

Every decision you delay out of fear has a cost. Not always visible, but always real. The cost of unearned growth. The cost of unrehearsed confidence. The cost of waiting to be sure in a system where certainty never arrives. The only antidote is action—small, repeatable, humble action. And once you take it, the fear equation starts to shift. What was once intimidating becomes navigable. What was once uncertain becomes familiar. And what was once feared becomes the very thing that expands your autonomy.

The Set-It-Up and Leave-It Framework

The most underrated wealth-building strategy available to everyday earners is not intelligence, luck, or even starting capital—it's design. A well-constructed, low-maintenance investment system, once set up, removes the daily burden of decision-making, outperforms most active strategies over time, and restores energy for higher-order thinking. The problem is not that people can't invest. It's that they're overwhelmed by choices, paralysed by jargon, and distracted by noise masquerading as opportunity. The antidote is not more information. It's structure. And the most effective structure for long-term investors is one that demands as little of their attention as possible.

When you automate intelligently, you sidestep one of the biggest liabilities in investing: human error. Studies in behavioural finance—from Barber and Odean's foundational research to more recent work on "behaviour gaps"—consistently show that *investors, not investments, are the problem.* We buy high, sell low, chase trends, and react emotionally to market dips. The more we interfere, the more we sabotage. The set-it-up and leave-it approach turns this insight into a strategic advantage by *designing out the need for willpower.*

At its core, this framework is built on three principles: simplicity, consistency, and invisibility. Simplicity means choosing vehicles that are transparent, diversified, and low-cost. For most readers, this means broad-based index funds—such as a FTSE All-World tracker or a globally diversified equity fund. These instruments don't require you to pick winners. They *are* the market. They adjust automatically as economies evolve, companies rise or fall, and sectors rotate. Rather than trying to outguess the system, you own the system—and you do so with minimal friction.

Consistency refers to regular contributions. You don't wait for the market to crash. You don't time the peaks. You choose a percentage of your income—say 10%—and invest it on the same day every month, regardless of headlines. This strategy, known as pound-cost averaging, reduces the emotional volatility of investing. When markets dip, your money buys more. When they rise, your earlier purchases compound. Over time, the discipline of regularity beats the anxiety of perfect timing.

Invisibility is where most frameworks falter. The best systems are not those you engage with daily—they're the ones that hum quietly in the background while you focus on living. The direct debit from your current account to your investment ISA. The pre-scheduled allocation between equities and bonds. The annual rebalance you calendar once and automate via your platform. These features make the system *functionally invisible.* You're not choosing every week to be disciplined—you've made one design decision that keeps paying off.

This structure isn't just convenient. It's transformative. Because it reduces financial thinking to a handful of strategic decisions per year, it liberates cognitive bandwidth. You're no longer reacting to market movements, reading investment gossip, or toggling between funds in search of marginally better returns. You've reclaimed your attention. And attention is a non-renewable resource—wasting it on minutiae is more damaging than most market downturns.

The psychological benefits compound just as powerfully as the financial ones. By automating your investing process, you eliminate one of the most corrosive dynamics in personal finance: the guilt of inconsistency. You're not checking balances obsessively. You're not wondering if you forgot to transfer this month. You're not stuck in a cycle of starting strong, losing steam, and starting again. Instead, *you've created a behaviourally intelligent system that works even when your motivation doesn't.*

Critics of passive automation often argue that it removes the possibility of higher returns. That's technically true—you won't beat the market. But most active investors don't either. The average investor underperforms the funds they invest in by 1–2% annually due to poor timing and emotional decisions. Compound that underperformance over 20 years and the results are staggering. Passive, automated investing isn't about settling for average returns—it's about *capturing actual returns*, not theoretical ones.

Still, many resist automation because it feels like surrendering control. But the opposite is true. Control isn't about micromanagement. It's about alignment. You're not delegating blindly—you're designing a system once that reflects your long-term values, risk tolerance, and income structure. And then you're letting it run. That's *real control*: not the illusion of mastery, but the quiet confidence of infrastructure.

A set-it-and-leave-it system is especially well-suited to readers who identify as neurodivergent, easily overwhelmed, or simply exhausted by constant financial vigilance. Not everyone enjoys spreadsheets, market analysis, or tinkering with accounts. Nor should they need to. The goal of wealth is not to become an amateur portfolio manager—it's to support a life of clarity and agency. If your investment strategy consumes more emotional energy than it returns in security, it's not working—even if it's technically sound.

This framework is not inflexible. Life evolves, and systems should adapt accordingly. If your income changes significantly, you can adjust your contributions. If your risk tolerance shifts—say, after having children or nearing retirement—you can adjust your asset allocation. But these are *deliberate calibrations*, not reactive tweaks. Your default is still stability, not reactivity.

Let's make this concrete. Suppose you're a salaried professional earning £45,000 annually. You set up a standing order to transfer £375 (10% of your income) into a stocks and shares ISA on the 1st of every month. Within that ISA, you've selected a single globally diversified index fund. You review your allocation once a year to rebalance if necessary. Everything else runs automatically. Over 15 years, assuming historical average returns of 6–7%, that system will build substantial capital—with almost no ongoing effort. *That is the power of automated simplicity.*

Now consider a self-employed reader. Irregular income can make fixed monthly investing harder. But you can design around that. Instead of a standing order, you set a policy: for every client payment, 10% goes directly into your investment account before anything else. You batch contributions weekly or fortnightly, aligning them with cash flow. The system still functions—it just adapts to your income rhythm. And you avoid the feast-or-famine trap that derails so many freelancers.

For those nearing retirement, the same framework applies with minor shifts. You may gradually introduce a bond allocation to reduce volatility. You may draw down a small percentage annually for living expenses. But the underlying system remains intact. *The goal was never to tinker—it was to trust.* And trust is earned through evidence: this approach works, and it works because it respects human nature, not because it tries to override it.

There's a deeper insight here, and it goes beyond finance. Most people don't fail because they lack knowledge. They fail because their systems are fragile. They depend on motivation, memory, or mood. But none of those are stable inputs. The beauty of a well-designed investment system is that it decouples performance from psychology. It replaces discipline with architecture. And in a world engineered for distraction, *that is one of the few sustainable competitive advantages left.*

The question isn't whether you could be a good investor. It's whether you've set yourself up to win even on your worst days. That's what the set-it-up and leave-it framework offers: not just wealth, but resilience. Not just automation, but peace. And in the long arc of financial independence, *peace is worth more than any extra yield.*

Chapter 8
Make Money a Relationship, Not a God

Money is not a measure of virtue. It does not reflect intelligence, character, or spiritual merit. Yet, in contemporary economies—especially those saturated with hyper-capitalist, achievement-oriented narratives—it is frequently treated as precisely that. For many, money has ceased to be a mere instrument of exchange or a vehicle for freedom; it has become a distorted mirror in which we assess our identity, status, and adequacy. We do not simply earn it—we worship it, fear it, chase it, and feel shame when it eludes us. This chapter intervenes not against money itself, but against the patterns of thought and emotion we have been conditioned to attach to it.

To extricate ourselves from this idolatry, we must first recognise how culture has framed money. Wealth is marketed not as a by-product of competent work or careful planning, but as a signifier of self-actualisation. In this narrative, money promises more than comfort; it offers salvation. It claims to end anxiety, prove value, and validate ambition. But this belief is corrosive. No figure, once reached, ever truly satisfies when used to patch a deeper sense of inadequacy. The question is not whether money matters—it does. The real question is how it should function in your life, and under what terms.

We propose a shift: from treating money as deity to engaging with it as dialogue. Money becomes something alive, responsive, and dynamic. Like any healthy relationship, clarity, boundaries, and honesty are essential. Your financial life should be a conversation, not a lecture, a source of shame, or an arbiter of your self-respect.

This repositioning is not indulgent—it is practical. When money functions as an omnipresent judge, every purchase becomes a moral referendum, every setback an existential crisis, and every discussion with a partner, friend, or colleague laden with defensiveness and avoidance. That is not financial literacy; it is a trauma loop. Sustainable wealth requires stepping out of that loop and into a relationship grounded in agency, awareness, and reflection.

Part of the challenge lies in inherited emotional scripts around money. These patterns are often invisible yet deeply entrenched. Some learn that money is never secure, that earnings can vanish at any moment. Others internalise the idea that caring about money is shallow or greedy. Some grow up in households where money sparks conflict, secrecy, or silence. These narratives persist into adulthood, frequently unnoticed yet consistently shaping behaviour, often more powerfully than any spreadsheet ever could.

This chapter addresses that reality head-on. We explore the intersection of money and mental health—not to pathologise, but to illuminate. Financial anxiety is rarely a mere budgeting problem; it can be a physiological response to scarcity or trauma. Overspending is not necessarily a failure of discipline but may be an attempt to regulate emotion in the absence of better tools. Avoidance is not laziness; it may be a self-protective strategy rooted in shame. Conditions like ADHD, depression, or chronic stress can further distort perception and interaction with financial reality. Understanding this complexity invites compassion, which is indispensable for meaningful behavioural change.

We also tackle a skill seldom taught to adults: how to converse about money. Conversations with partners, parents, roommates, or friends are often minefields—not due to dishonesty but inexperience. Vulnerability is mistaken for weakness, fear of judgment clouds communication. This chapter provides practical frameworks and scripts, rooted in psychology and communication theory, to navigate money discussions with clarity, honesty, and minimal conflict. Speaking candidly about finances is a core life skill, not a luxury.

Perhaps the most transformative exercise in this chapter is also the quietest: writing your money vows. This is not a branding ritual; it is a means of alignment. Just as marriage vows articulate a sacred commitment, money vows define your ethical, emotional, and strategic stance toward wealth. What do you stand for financially? What will you not compromise? Which fears are you naming, and which aspirations honouring? These vows act as a compass when making career moves, investment choices, lifestyle decisions, or responding to setbacks. They do not simplify decisions but make them coherent.

Why does this matter? No amount of external wealth compensates for internal disarray. Without clarity, financial milestones and pay rises merely amplify the same anxious self. The solution is not rejecting ambition but de-idolising income, allowing wealth to support clarity, dignity, and freedom rather than anxiety and over-identification.

As you progress through this chapter, there will be no "fixes" offered, no prescriptive formulas to download. True financial clarity is designed iteratively, reflecting who you are and what you value. Our role is to illuminate obstacles to that clarity and provide tools, language, and insight to render the invisible visible.

Ultimately, treating money as a relationship rather than a god is an act of sovereignty. It declares that your worth is not determined by net worth, your future is not dictated by your past, and your bank balance does not define you. You become the architect of a financial life that embodies your deepest convictions. This is not a motivational slogan—it is a design principle: simple, repeatable, and quietly revolutionary.

Stop Worshiping, Start Relating:

In many modern cultures, money has taken on a metaphysical role it was never meant to play. It is no longer simply a tool for exchange or a measure of stored value—it has become a social litmus test, a psychological crutch, a moral validator. We speak of financial success with the hushed reverence once reserved for spiritual enlightenment. But unlike religion, which at its best offers meaning, structure, and humility, money as worship delivers anxiety, competition, and a distorted sense of self. The issue is not that we value money too much—it's that we relate to it in ways that are incoherent, compulsive, and emotionally hollow.

This is not a screed against wealth. It's a critique of *confusing net worth with self-worth*, and of outsourcing meaning to metrics that can never provide it. For the upwardly mobile professional, the temptation is subtle but persistent: to use money as a mirror, hoping it will eventually reflect back competence, status, and finally, peace. But the more we chase validation through accumulation, the more we entrench ourselves in an identity that is both fragile and exhausting. If money becomes your proxy for power, security, or love, then it will also become your permanent source of fear—because anything that can be gained can be lost, and anything external can be manipulated or withheld.

This dynamic is amplified by the architecture of the attention economy. Every scroll through social media presents a highlight reel of curated affluence—productivity influencers selling digital hustle fantasies, financial gurus flaunting crypto profits, and peers casually posting from rooftop bars in borrowed outfits. The message is implicit but clear: *You should have more by now.* But the real danger isn't the envy such content provokes; it's the internalised shame it produces. When money becomes the default scoreboard of adulthood, it's easy to start living for optics rather than alignment. You begin optimising for admiration rather than fulfilment.

What's required is a full recalibration—not of ambition, but of relationship. Instead of exalting money as a symbol of ultimate achievement, we must bring it back down to its rightful place: a vital but morally neutral resource. This begins with identifying how we've been taught to *relate* to money, often unconsciously. For some, money was always scarce, tightly rationed and emotionally loaded. For others, it came easily, but with strings attached—conditional love, silent expectations, or subtle manipulation. These early emotional associations become the architecture of our adult financial behaviour. We repeat patterns not because they're rational, but because they're familiar.

To build a healthier relationship with money, we must surface these scripts and interrogate them with clarity and compassion. What emotions do you associate with spending? Guilt, fear, excitement, control? What do you believe people will think of you if you earn a lot—or if you don't? These are not theoretical questions. They are diagnostic tools. Because *until you understand how you've been trained to feel about money, you'll continue to act on those feelings without knowing why*.

Relating to money rather than worshipping it means acknowledging its power without letting it define you. It means holding two truths simultaneously: that money impacts everything from housing to healthcare, but that it should influence your values—not replace them. When money becomes your god, every decision becomes transactional. But when money becomes your partner, you begin making decisions that are expressive, principled, and strategic.

This is not merely semantics. Consider how this shift plays out in real life. The person who worships money asks, *"How much can I earn?"*The person who relates to money asks, *"What am I building, and why?"* The worshipper hoards out of fear, convinced that safety lies in accumulation. The relational thinker allocates with intentionality, understanding that security comes not just from having, but from *knowing how to use.* One builds a fortress. The other builds a framework.

Even the language we use reveals our relational posture. Saying "I can't afford that" often masks something deeper—either fear of scarcity or internalised guilt. A more accurate, empowered phrase might be, "That's not how I'm choosing to allocate resources right now." This simple linguistic shift signals agency. It suggests that you're not at the mercy of your finances, but actively in dialogue with them.

This reframing also helps us resist the binary thinking that dominates financial discourse. You don't have to choose between spiritual depth and material competence. You can want more money *and* care deeply about justice. You can build wealth *and* reject greed. You can be ambitious *and* content. False dichotomies arise when money is placed on a pedestal and stripped of its context. But when we relate to money as one dimension of a full, complex life, we allow ourselves to hold multiple identities at once: earner, giver, builder, learner, citizen, parent, friend.

Of course, this relational approach to money isn't naturalised by intention alone. It must be practiced. This means regular check-ins with your financial life—not to obsess, but to orient. Ask: *Is my spending aligned with my stated values? Are my goals self-authored, or inherited from someone else's script? Am I making financial decisions from fear, habit, or clarity?* These are the kinds of reflective questions that shift your money posture from reaction to response, from reactivity to relationship.

What's radical about this approach is that it invites *enoughness* back into the conversation. Not as a retreat from aspiration, but as a rebuke to the idea that you must continually prove your legitimacy by levelling up your lifestyle. If you've ever experienced the odd disappointment of reaching a financial milestone only to feel unmoved by it, you've glimpsed the truth: *Without a relational foundation, no amount will satisfy.* This doesn't mean you stop earning, building, or striving. It means you stop doing those things for approval you no longer need.

A relational model of money also softens interpersonal dynamics. When you no longer treat money as sacred, it becomes easier to talk about—especially in the context of relationships. It becomes a topic of mutual exploration, not hierarchy. Whether negotiating a shared budget with a partner or discussing salary with a colleague, conversations grounded in honesty and humility become not just possible, but fruitful. The goal is not perfection, but fluency.

Ultimately, to stop worshipping money and start relating to it is to reclaim authorship over your financial life. It is to say: I refuse to let arbitrary metrics, inherited scripts, or cultural noise dictate what I value, how I live, or who I become. This is not a rejection of wealth. It is a reassertion of sovereignty. When money ceases to be your master, it can finally become your ally—and that shift, subtle but seismic, may be the most important transformation of all.

Money and Mental Health:

Most people believe they have a "money problem." Fewer recognise that what they have is a *nervous system problem* masquerading as a budgeting issue. The impulse to overspend, under-earn, avoid, hoard, or obsess rarely originates from ignorance. It comes from somewhere deeper: anxiety, shame, trauma, compulsivity, or even grief. When the conversation around money ignores mental health, it promotes strategies that collapse under the weight of emotional reality. And yet, this remains one of the most neglected areas in financial literature—where spreadsheets dominate and psyche is sidelined. That omission is not just inadequate; it's irresponsible.

We are not born with financial behaviours. We inherit them. We absorb them through family patterns, social environments, media conditioning, and neurobiological wiring. For many, their first experience of money was not about numbers, but *emotions*—a parent's panic at a credit card statement, a scarcity-driven argument over bills, or the subtle but steady tension of never quite having enough. These early scripts don't stay in childhood. They evolve into adult habits: avoidance, under-earning, impulsivity, financial hypervigilance. And critically, these aren't irrational. They're adaptations—often intelligent ones. If your nervous system associates money with instability or shame, your behaviours around it will reflect not greed or laziness, but a bid for emotional safety.

Consider ADHD—a condition often trivialised as mere distractibility. In financial life, its consequences are profound: missed due dates, forgotten subscriptions, inconsistent income streams, decision fatigue. Executive dysfunction isn't a character flaw; it's a cognitive reality that disrupts planning, foresight, and follow-through. When financial systems are designed only for neurotypical patterns, they set others up for failure, and then blame them for falling behind. What's needed isn't more discipline, but *design.* Systems that remove friction, reduce decisions, and accommodate fluctuation create dignity, not just structure.

Similarly, those with trauma histories often engage in financial behaviour that looks self-defeating—until it's understood through a psychological lens. Trauma, especially complex or developmental trauma, disrupts a person's sense of time. It makes the future feel abstract or even unsafe. If tomorrow doesn't feel real, then planning for retirement feels irrelevant. The choice to spend today, even recklessly, isn't necessarily about pleasure—it's often a survival response. Financial advice that ignores this dimension fails not because it's incorrect, but because it's emotionally tone-deaf.

Depression introduces its own distortions. It can turn the simplest financial task—checking a balance, logging into an account—into a mountain of dread. Energy becomes so scarce that shame compounds over every delayed payment or unopened envelope. The common suggestion to "just face it" doesn't land. What's required is *scaffolding*: low-stakes, emotionally safe ways to re-engage with your money without triggering shutdown. This could mean building rituals around reviewing finances in calming settings, linking money tasks to pleasurable habits, or having an accountability partner who offers support without judgement. The goal is not just functionality—it's emotional re-entry.

Anxiety, by contrast, can manifest as overcontrol. For some, it fuels compulsive budgeting, obsessive saving, or relentless financial monitoring. On the surface, these behaviours look responsible—even admirable. But beneath them often lies a relentless fear: of loss, of regression, of being unprepared for catastrophe. The person is not financially prudent; they are *hypervigilant*. Their spreadsheets are not tools—they are shields. The trouble is that anxiety-driven control rarely delivers the safety it promises. Instead, it narrows one's life, turning freedom into a mirage always one savings goal away.

Mental health also shapes how we *interpret* financial events. A late payment might mean inconvenience to one person, and failure to another. A small raise might bring joy to someone else, and shame to the person who believes they should be "further ahead." Perception is not a luxury here—it's a determinant. And these perceptions are not simply changed through logic. They shift through reframing, healing, and sometimes professional intervention. That's why any serious approach to personal finance must move beyond tactics and into the terrain of identity, emotion, and mental health.

None of this is an argument for financial fatalism. Quite the opposite. It's a case for *financial frameworks that integrate psychological insight with practical action*. Strategies that accommodate energy fluctuations. Systems that prioritise emotional sustainability alongside mathematical soundness. Language that normalises struggle without glorifying stagnation. And most of all, financial education that recognises this simple truth: *your money life is inseparable from your emotional life*.

There's also a collective aspect we must name. Western culture, particularly in its capitalist expressions, tends to pathologise financial struggle as a personal failure. But financial difficulty is often the predictable result of systemic pressure: wage stagnation, precarious employment, healthcare costs, racial and gender inequities, neurodivergent invisibility. To talk about money without acknowledging these forces is to misrepresent the problem—and misprescribe the solution. Healing, in this context, is not just about private reflection. It's also about advocacy, boundaries, and structural awareness.

It's worth mentioning that not all financial mental health work is clinical. Some of the most transformative shifts come from simple yet profound redefinitions. Redefining success not as constant accumulation, but as alignment. Redefining enough not as a minimum standard, but as a moving, relational threshold. Redefining discipline not as rigidity, but as compassionate consistency. These shifts don't just change behaviour—they change worldview.

For example, instead of viewing budgeting as self-deprivation, reframing it as *resource stewardship* can feel empowering rather than punitive. Instead of viewing debt as a moral failing, understanding it as a contextual reality—sometimes a strategic bridge, sometimes an outcome of constrained choices—allows for action without shame. Instead of treating financial goals as pressure cookers, treating them as *curated priorities* shifts the tone from obligation to authorship.

There is immense relief in this kind of reframe. It breaks the binary of "get your act together or suffer the consequences," and introduces a more human, humane alternative: *learn your nervous system, understand your history, build from where you are, not where you're supposed to be.* This doesn't let us off the hook from responsibility—it grounds our responsibility in reality. And reality, while messy, is always more manageable than shame.

Practically speaking, this means curating a money system that works with, not against, your psychological profile. If you know you struggle with executive function, automate your bills, set visual reminders, or link key actions to routine behaviours. If you know anxiety drives your spending, build in delay mechanisms—like a 24-

hour rule for purchases—so your emotions don't hijack your decisions. If shame is paralysing you from opening your bank app, consider doing it in a low-stress environment with someone you trust beside you. These are not hacks. They are relational gestures—toward yourself, and your future.

Importantly, the work of integrating money and mental health isn't a one-time event. It's cyclical, adaptive, and requires ongoing self-awareness. Life events—job changes, diagnoses, relationships, loss—will continually shift your mental health and, by extension, your financial tendencies. The goal is not to reach a perfect state, but to cultivate fluency: the ability to read your own patterns, to adjust proactively, and to respond with care rather than criticism.

What emerges from this work is not just financial literacy—but financial *resilience.* Not just competence, but congruence. You stop trying to imitate what works for others, and instead design systems, routines, and mindsets that honour how *you* operate. You give yourself permission to succeed in ways that are emotionally sustainable. And in doing so, you redefine what it means to be "good with money"—not as someone who always gets it right, but as someone who builds a relationship with it that is informed, intentional, and self-respecting. That kind of relationship doesn't just increase wealth. It restores dignity.

Financial Conversations That Don't Suck:

Few topics trigger more tension, evasion, or awkwardness than money. For many, it ranks somewhere between dental surgery and unsolicited feedback in terms of conversational dread. Yet our financial lives are inseparable from our relationships. The way we spend, save, share, or withhold money is deeply intertwined with trust, values, power, and identity. And still, we rarely discuss it with clarity or care. When we do, it often happens under duress—during conflict, after a mistake, or on the brink of major decisions. The result is predictably messy: miscommunication, defensiveness, and often, silence that calcifies into long-term mistrust. But it doesn't have to be this way. Financial conversations are a skill. And like any skill, they can be designed, practiced, and improved—not to perform politeness, but to build real intimacy and understanding.

The first myth worth dismantling is that talking about money is inherently uncomfortable. It's not. *What makes it uncomfortable is the lack of structure, clarity, and shared language.* Most people were not raised in environments where money was discussed openly. Silence was the norm, or worse, tension-filled arguments set the tone. So when adulthood demands these conversations—between partners, friends, or family—we carry forward emotional scripts that sabotage us before we've even begun. The shame, guilt, or secrecy we inherited becomes the filter through which every financial discussion is interpreted. Neutral facts feel like criticisms. Simple questions feel like interrogations. The conversation collapses because the foundation was never solid to begin with.

Effective financial dialogue starts with reframing: *money isn't just numbers—it's meaning.* When someone says they "can't afford" something, they may be articulating a financial constraint. But they may also be communicating fear, values, priorities, or relational power. Likewise, when someone avoids discussing debt, they're not being irresponsible—they may be protecting themselves from shame or judgement. Financial behaviours are always downstream of emotion. That's why a productive money conversation doesn't start with "How much do you make?" It starts with "What does financial security mean to you?" or "What were you taught to believe about money growing up?" These questions don't just uncover facts—they reveal context.

In romantic partnerships, financial transparency is often mistaken for compatibility. But transparency without mutual understanding can backfire. Consider the couple where one partner tracks every expenditure down to the penny, while the other lives by an intuitive sense of balance. On paper, their goals may align—save for a home, invest for the future—but their *styles* clash dramatically. One experiences security through precision; the other through fluidity. If this isn't surfaced early, the friction will surface eventually—through passive aggression, resentment, or covert behaviour. A useful practice here is what some therapists call a "Money Origin Story" exercise. Each partner independently writes a short reflection on how their early experiences with money—good, bad, or absent—shaped their current habits. Sharing this openly builds empathy, not just knowledge. It reframes differences as inherited strategies, not character flaws.

Friendship adds another layer of complexity. Money often creates invisible power dynamics that no one acknowledges until it's too late. One friend consistently pays more when splitting bills. Another feels excluded from group activities due to budget constraints but is too embarrassed to speak up. These micro-tensions erode connection over time. Here, *normalising transparency before it's urgent* is crucial. For example, a friend suggesting, "Let's plan something fun that doesn't cost much—my budget's tight this month," models vulnerability without drama. Or during group planning, someone asking, "What's a budget everyone's comfortable with?" creates space for equity without shame. These moves aren't just polite—they're strategic. They set a tone where financial difference isn't taboo, it's just one more variable to coordinate respectfully.

Within families, money is often laced with unspoken expectations and legacy roles. The eldest child may be expected to support parents. A high-earning sibling may feel guilted into bailing others out. An inheritance conversation may never happen until it's too late. Families tend to default to either secrecy or control—both of which block trust. In this context, *timing, tone, and intention* matter deeply. A conversation about estate planning isn't just about assets—it's about autonomy, fairness, and legacy. Avoiding it doesn't protect relationships—it endangers them. One entry point might be something like: "I've been thinking about how we as a family handle money decisions long-term. I'd love to hear your thoughts on how we approach that proactively rather than reactively." The key is to anchor the conversation in shared values—care, fairness, responsibility—not individual outcomes.

What makes these conversations successful isn't perfect wording. It's *emotional tone and conversational structure*. A well-structured financial dialogue tends to include three things: context, curiosity, and collaboration. First, **context**: explain why you're raising the topic now, and what you hope the conversation achieves. For instance: "We've been thinking about moving in together, and I realised we haven't really talked about how we'll handle expenses. I'd love for us to be aligned so it feels fair and clear for both of us." Second,

curiosity: ask open-ended questions and truly listen. Resist the urge to fix, correct, or defend. Third, **collaboration**: work toward a shared decision or plan, rather than issuing demands or ultimatums. Instead of "You need to stop spending so much," try "Can we look together at how our spending aligns with what we both value most right now?"

When conflict does arise—and it will—the goal isn't to win the argument. It's to *stay connected while addressing the tension.* That means managing tone, separating facts from interpretations, and sometimes taking breaks when things escalate. Statements like "I'm noticing I'm feeling defensive—can we pause and come back to this later?" are not signs of failure. They're signs of maturity. Avoiding money fights is not the goal. Learning to move through them constructively is.

Scripts can help when language feels like a barrier. Here are a few examples tailored for common scenarios:

— **Initiating a conversation about shared expenses with a partner:**
"I'd love for us to revisit how we're handling money stuff—just to make sure we're both feeling good about it. No pressure to change anything immediately, but I think having clarity could help us avoid future stress."

— **Addressing discomfort in a group setting:**
"Hey, I'd love to join the plan for this weekend, but my budget's a bit tight. Could we think of something a little less pricey, or I'll catch you all next time?"

— **Navigating financial support with family:**
"I want to support where I can, and also need to make sure I'm not stretching beyond what's sustainable. Can we talk about expectations and maybe look at other ways I can be helpful too?"

The goal of these scripts isn't to eliminate emotion. It's to channel it productively. Money is always emotional. But *clear, compassionate structure* allows emotion to inform, not hijack, the conversation.

Beyond words, it's also helpful to build *regular rhythms* for financial communication. Waiting until things go wrong creates pressure and defensiveness. Instead, establish low-stakes, recurring check-ins: a monthly "money date" with a partner, an annual review with family members involved in shared finances, or even a quarterly financial reflection solo or with a friend. These rituals de-escalate urgency and normalise transparency. Over time, they transform financial conversation from a crisis response into a practice of connection.

We tend to treat money as a private matter—something to master alone, in silence. But that framework isolates us. It magnifies shame, reduces accountability, and deprives us of wisdom. When we instead treat money as a *relational practice*, it becomes not just manageable, but meaningful. It becomes a domain where trust is built, not broken. Where intimacy is deepened, not avoided. And where values are enacted, not just imagined.

Financial fluency is more than understanding numbers. It's learning how to speak—*and listen*—in a language that aligns money with care, clarity, and collective integrity. That's not just a communication skill. It's a life skill. And one of the most transformative you'll ever learn.

Writing Your New Money Vows:

Most people inherit their relationship with money by accident. It's shaped not by deliberate reflection but by exposure—through parents' arguments, cultural scripts, early anxieties, and moments of deprivation or indulgence. Over time, this patchwork solidifies into habits, often unconscious, that govern financial decisions for decades. And yet, if you ask most individuals what they *believe* about money, what role it plays in their life, or how they define enough, few can answer with clarity. They're navigating one of the most consequential forces in modern life without a compass. Writing new money vows changes that. It transforms financial decision-making from reactive to principled, from scattered to centred.

The idea is not metaphorical. A vow is a promise—but not just any promise. It is chosen, intentional, and identity-rooted. Vows bind us not just to behaviours, but to *principles*. They name the values we want to express consistently through action, even under pressure. Just as personal vows in a relationship orient us during conflict, fatigue, or change, money vows help us hold direction amid temptation, comparison, or uncertainty. *They reduce cognitive noise and decision fatigue by providing a stable set of criteria through which trade-offs become legible.*

Why does this matter? Because the financial world is not short on information. Anyone can google a budgeting app, investment guide, or mortgage calculator. What people lack is *alignment.* Alignment between their behaviours and their beliefs. Between their goals and their values. Between their desires and their definitions of enough. Without this alignment, people accumulate tactics without traction. They optimise without introspection. They mimic without meaning. The result is often confusion that masquerades as productivity: more spreadsheets, more dashboards, but less clarity about what actually matters.

The process of crafting money vows begins with one essential premise: *money is a mirror, not a measure.* It reflects what we prioritise, what we fear, and what we believe about control, security, generosity, and self-worth. This reflection can be distorted—by trauma, scarcity, or cultural messaging—but that only makes the case stronger for conscious redesign. When we write new vows, we are not just setting intentions for the future; we are interrogating the defaults we've been living under. This is not self-help fluff. It's financial epistemology. It asks: What do I truly know about what money means in my life—and what have I merely assumed?

Take, for example, someone raised in a household where money was unstable. Their learned vow, though never spoken, may have been: *I will never depend on anyone else again.* This vow might drive admirable independence—but it might also block collaboration, trust, or risk-taking that could serve them now. Another person may have absorbed the idea that *spending on others is love.* That too carries both warmth and danger. The key is not to judge these internal scripts, but to surface and revise them.

To do this well, the process should begin with reflection, not prescription. One effective prompt is: *"When have I felt most financially at peace?"* Followed by: *"When have I felt most financially anxious, ashamed, or resentful?"* The contrast between these moments reveals more than numbers ever will. It reveals *drivers*: control, freedom, status, belonging, fear. These emotional anchors are the substructure beneath every budget, investment, or negotiation. Naming them is not indulgent—it's necessary.

Next comes articulation. A good money vow is neither vague nor dogmatic. It is specific enough to guide, yet spacious enough to adapt. "I will never go into debt again" is brittle—it doesn't allow for strategic borrowing (like a mortgage or a business investment). "I value financial freedom" is too abstract to drive action. But "I will use debt only when it expands long-term autonomy, not short-term relief" strikes the right balance. It's directional, contextual, and grounded in a principle.

Vows can address different domains. Some will orient around spending: *"I will not use consumption to mask emotional avoidance."* Others may centre saving: *"I save not out of fear, but out of respect for future possibilities."* Others still may focus on generosity: *"I give with discernment, not obligation—and never at the cost of my own stability."* The point is not to create a manifesto, but a compass. A handful of thoughtful vows—five, perhaps—is more useful than a sprawling declaration. Each vow should feel like a stake in the ground: a reference point you return to when tempted, afraid, or lost.

One common resistance to this exercise is that life is unpredictable. How can a fixed set of vows account for changing circumstances, evolving goals, or shifting relationships? The answer is they're not *fixed*—they're *foundational.* Just as core values in a marriage don't preclude change, but rather support it, financial vows are adaptable. They're not meant to predict the future; they're meant to protect your integrity as the future unfolds. Without them, you are far more vulnerable to decision fatigue, external pressure, or impulsive choices driven by emotion rather than clarity.

The impact of money vows extends beyond the personal. They enhance conversations, align relationships, and anchor negotiations. A couple who has shared vows such as "We will prioritise freedom over status" or "We will be transparent about our fears before making big decisions" enters a budget meeting with an entirely different posture. It's not about defending transactions—it's about honouring shared commitments. Likewise, a solo entrepreneur who has vowed "I will build systems that scale, not just work harder" will make very different business decisions than one driven only by urgency or revenue.

It's also worth noting that vows are not just about restraint—they are about permission. Many people who have internalised scarcity or shame around money benefit enormously from vows that affirm their right to enjoy, to rest, or to invest in themselves. For example: *"I am allowed to experience pleasure without guilt when it's in alignment with my values."* Or: *"I will not defer my life until some arbitrary financial milestone is reached."* These are not loopholes. They are acts of balance. And balance is not moral compromise—it's the condition for sustainability.

Once written, money vows must be visible. Hidden vows lose their power. Keep them where you can review them periodically—in a journal, a notes app, or even on your calendar. Set a quarterly reminder to reread and reflect: Are these still true? Are they being honoured? Are they producing clarity? If not, revise. A vow that can't be re-examined becomes a rule. And rules, without reflection, become dogma.

For those seeking to build their first $100k—and beyond—this exercise isn't a distraction from strategy. It *is* strategy. Because strategies are only as effective as the principles behind them. You can choose the best savings account, the smartest index fund, or the optimal side hustle. But if your financial behaviour is misaligned with your values, the results will always feel hollow, or worse, self-sabotaging. *Money vows close that gap.* They turn scattered knowledge into coherent identity. They transform money from an instrument of anxiety into an instrument of agency.

Ultimately, this is not about perfection. You will still make mistakes, face uncertainty, and revise your plans. But with well-crafted vows, you will do so from a place of integrity. Not just chasing outcomes, but *living a philosophy.* And in a world constantly trying to sell you someone else's priorities, that is a radically powerful thing to do.

Chapter 9
Designing Your Financial Life

The point of wealth is rarely the accumulation itself; it is the careful shaping of a life that fits you, rather than the other way around. Yet most people—racing toward financial freedom—never pause to define what freedom truly means for them. Money is treated as a metric of success rather than as a tool for design. The consequence is a life lived on autopilot: income rises, expenses follow, obligations mount—and fulfilment remains stubbornly out of reach. The central aim of this chapter is to reclaim design as the organising principle of personal finance. Not decoration, but deliberate structure: the thoughtful construction of a life that reflects your values, rhythms, curiosities, and priorities.

This is not about the superficial upgrades of lifestyle—it is about lifestyle architecture. How should your days feel once money no longer dictates choices? Where would you live, how would you work, which relationships merit investment, which risks are worth taking, and what might you stop apologising for? These questions are not abstractions reserved for retirement; they are design parameters that can be reverse-engineered into the present. Without a blueprint, financial growth is arbitrary; you may end up optimising for outcomes you do not truly desire.

Intentional design begins long before wealth accumulates. Indeed, its most potent forms often emerge under constraint. Someone earning a modest salary yet structuring life around low-cost community, part-time creative work, or flexible geography may experience a richer sense of autonomy than a six-figure earner trapped in an office-rent-commute treadmill. Autonomy is not a function of income—it is a function of alignment. Alignment where money, time, and values reinforce rather than compete. This chapter explores practical strategies for creating that alignment, even before major financial milestones arrive.

A key framework here is the concept of long bets. In investing, long-term positions are lauded for compounding returns; in life, long bets are often underappreciated. These are deliberate decisions made today that quietly yield exponential benefit over time. Building a personal brand in your twenties. Moving to a city with a slower pace and stronger community. Pursuing a side project whose rewards may take years to materialise but that enlarges your creative autonomy. Such bets can appear inefficient in the short term, yet they are the foundation of extraordinary lives. Design is not about maximising immediate efficiency—it is about cultivating leverage for the person you aim to become.

Many face a more subtle challenge: a surfeit of noise. Everywhere, algorithms dictate what success should look like—exotic travel, minimalist interiors, passive income screenshots, the perfectly curated calendar. Strip away this digital theatre and what remains? Which parts of your lifestyle are genuinely chosen, and which are inherited, imitated, or nudged by unseen code? Financial design is an act of authorship. It demands stepping out of algorithmic mimicry and into sovereign decision-making. The question shifts from "what is possible?" to "what is worthwhile?"

This chapter does not offer a blueprint for someone else's ideal life; it sharpens the lens on your own. We guide you through designing deliberately under real constraints. Filtering financial decisions not merely through spreadsheets but through values. Letting go of status-driven upgrades in favour of self-defined priorities. Evaluating trade-offs with a strategist's eye rather than a consumer's impulse. Most importantly, building a system that reinforces your agency rather than eroding it.

We also address detaching wealth from performance metrics. Many equate productivity with worth, optimisation with progress. Yet a deeper form of design exists: one that prioritises peace, dignity, spaciousness, and quiet confidence unswayed by external validation. Freedom beyond the algorithm. Financial independence should not demand performance, nor submission to digital aesthetics. True wealth is existential: the ability to choose your rhythms, inputs, pace, and path without seeking permission or applause.

Every financial choice carries dual dimensions: numerical and narrative. Numbers matter, undeniably. But the underlying question is: what kind of life does this enable? A raise is not merely a figure; it redefines the obligations of your time. A relocation is not just a postcode; it reconfigures your social, mental, and emotional context. A savings target is not simply a sum; it signals what future pleasures you are willing to defer. Viewing money through a design lens transforms it from a separate concern into the very architecture of life in motion.

Designing your life, like any form of authorship, requires imagination and iteration. You may get it wrong at first. You may construct a lifestyle that suits ambition but strains your nervous system. That is data, not failure. The aim is not perfection but authorship. Too often, people outsource the structure of their lives to career ladders, consumer culture, or social media archetypes—then wonder why success feels hollow. Designing your financial life breaks that cycle.

This chapter provides practical tools for doing so: intentional budgeting aligned with actual priorities, lifestyle experiments that surface hidden preferences, decision-making frameworks that prioritise long-term alignment over short-term validation. We dismantle inherited assumptions about what makes a life "worth" the money, and offer methods to evaluate progress on your own terms, not the internet's.

What emerges is not a formula but a posture: life as design rather than reaction. Money as medium, not master. Success as structural coherence—the quiet, profound satisfaction of living in a manner that feels unmistakably, unshakably your own. That is the true payoff: not merely the first $100K, but a life that maintains its shape under pressure. A life designed, not defaulted.

Don't Just Grow—Shape It:

Growth, by itself, is directionless. You can grow a bank balance, grow a career, grow a business—and still end up somewhere you never intended to go. In personal finance, the word *growth* is treated as a universal good. But growth without intentionality becomes accumulation for accumulation's sake. The more pressing question is: *what is this growth in service of?* Not rhetorically, but concretely. When the numbers start to go up—your income, investments, options—what do you want that to *enable*? The mistake most people make is deferring this question until they've "made it." By then, they've often built a life optimised for metrics, not meaning.

This chapter invites a different approach. Start with shape, not scale. Ask what a well-lived life looks like *before* the wealth arrives, and build your financial systems to support that outcome from the start. Too many financial strategies mimic the logic of industrial production: more is better, bigger is safer, speed equals success. But humans aren't machines, and lives aren't assembly lines. *The goal is not infinite expansion; the goal is congruence.* When your income, time, values, and lived experience align—not just financially, but emotionally and structurally.

One of the most overlooked truths in personal finance is this: the richest decisions are often made when money is still tight. Why? Because constraints force clarity. When you can't afford everything, you're forced to choose what matters most. That's where shape emerges. Someone earning £35,000 a year who lives in a walkable city with free afternoons and meaningful friendships may be living closer to their ideal life than a high earner locked in a 70-hour workweek in a city they hate. *Freedom is not just about more money—it's about fewer misalignments.*

Yet the prevailing culture pushes us to delay lifestyle design until later. "Just work hard for now," the logic goes, "and design your life once you're financially secure." But that's backwards. *Financial security should be the byproduct of a well-designed life, not a prerequisite for it.* This isn't idealism. It's strategy. When you shape your lifestyle around sustainable habits, intentional choices, and values-aligned trade-offs, you're not just surviving—you're compounding. The early years of your financial life are not just about accumulation; they're about architecture. What you build now—your routines, relationships, identity structures—will calcify over time. So the question isn't just "how much can I grow?" but "what structure am I reinforcing as I grow?"

To do this well requires a form of reverse engineering. Start by asking: if you could design your days from scratch, what would they look like? Not in the abstract, but in texture. What time would you wake up? Who would you spend time with? What work would energise you? What would you *stop* doing? How would you move your body, fuel your brain, rest your nervous system? What risks would you take if your income didn't have to prove your worth? These questions aren't indulgent. They're clarifying. *Designing your financial life without asking them is like building a house without architectural plans.*

Let's make this more tangible. Consider someone working full-time in a high-pressure corporate role, earning well but exhausted. They dream of running their own consultancy with part-time hours and location independence. The traditional model says: save up, quit later. But a shaped approach asks: how can we start folding that future into the present? Could they negotiate a four-day week? Start freelancing on weekends? Build a reputation in a niche on LinkedIn? These aren't just income moves—they're *alignment moves.* They turn financial life into a creative medium, not a linear climb.

This isn't about sudden reinvention. It's about subtle reshaping. One hour a day spent writing, instead of scrolling. One bill negotiated lower, freeing up cash for a language class. One social event skipped, replaced by dinner with someone who inspires you. These micro-adjustments compound. They reshape identity. They make the future feel more proximate—and in doing so, they make financial discipline easier. *It's far easier to save for a life you've already started tasting.*

There's also a cognitive shift that must happen. Most people are trained to think about money in terms of sacrifice and scarcity: "I can't afford that," "I need to wait until," "I have to hold off." But the better frame is strategic reallocation. If your vision is clear, you're not denying yourself—you're investing in coherence. A smaller flat for more travel. Fewer subscriptions for more creative freedom. Less status signalling for more peace. *Every financial decision becomes a vote for the life you actually want.*

To get there, you need to start making decisions with your future self in the room. Not a fantasy self with no constraints, but a vivid, grounded version of who you're becoming. What do they prioritise? What do they regret not doing sooner? What invisible costs are they no longer willing to pay—constant stress, fragmented focus, performing success for others? Financial shape begins with this kind of dialogic honesty. Growth is easy to measure. Alignment is not. But the long-term cost of neglecting it is far greater.

In shaping your financial life, trade-offs are inevitable. That's not the problem. The problem is making them unconsciously, or by default. Should you live in a cheaper city to work fewer hours? Should you downsize to spend more on experiences? Should you delay income growth to learn a skill that'll give you 10x returns later? These are design questions, not budgeting ones. And there are no universally right answers—only *right-for-you* answers. That's why values clarity matters more than financial modelling.

We've been conditioned to think that financial design is what happens once we've "made it." But if you wait until you have money to decide who you want to be, money will decide for you. You'll default to the cultural templates: more stuff, more obligation, more performance. Designing from the inside-out flips that script. It says: define enough *before* you start chasing more. Build constraints *before* the world imposes them. Choose your metrics *before* the market does.

What you're really shaping is your *attention architecture*. Because time, not money, is your scarcest resource. And the more money you make, the more demands will compete for that time. If your financial systems are built around attention—not just accumulation—you stay in control. You choose what gets your mornings, your energy, your creativity. You build a life that doesn't require escape, because you've consciously shaped its core.

This article is not an argument against growth. It's an argument for growth that *points somewhere.* Income is leverage. Investing is wise. Wealth is useful. But none of it is meaningful until you decide what kind of life you want to live *with it.* The tragedy is not failing to grow—it's growing into a shape that doesn't fit you.

Designing your financial life means reintroducing authorship. Not just in theory, but in infrastructure. It means interrogating default assumptions and building something that reflects who you are and where you want to go. This is not a one-time exercise. It is an ongoing practice—a kind of financial choreography where every step reinforces the rhythm of your deeper priorities. The world will offer you countless templates for success. Your job is to decline most of them.

Because the goal isn't to win someone else's game. It's to shape a life that *doesn't require one.*

Lifestyle Design on a Budget:

Most people postpone lifestyle design until they believe they can "afford" it. They imagine it as a luxury—something that begins once they've crossed an invisible income threshold. The truth is, that moment often never comes. As income grows, so do expectations, obligations, and the inertia of routine. By the time people feel financially "ready" to design their lives, they've already outsourced most of their preferences to culture, convenience, or default norms. The opportunity is not to wait, but to start shaping your life while resources are still limited. Not as a compromise—but as an advantage. *Constraint sharpens creativity. Scarcity can, paradoxically, bring clarity.*

Lifestyle design is not a synonym for expensive tastes or exotic escapes. It is a method of aligning your environment, time, habits, relationships, and work around values that matter. You do not need a windfall to make better choices about where you live, how you work, who you spend time with, and what you prioritise. You need self-awareness, experimentation, and the discipline to reject what doesn't serve your larger vision. The most meaningful shifts in lifestyle often require *less* money, not more—because they trade excess for intentionality.

Consider location. Where you live shapes nearly every dimension of your daily life: your commute, your expenses, your community, your mental load. Yet most people choose it based on superficial prestige, proximity to their job, or family pressure. What if you inverted the logic? What if you started with lifestyle qualities—walkability, natural beauty, community cohesion, cultural fit—and then chose a location that supported those, even if it meant a smaller flat, a slower pace, or a different career mix? People routinely spend tens of thousands annually on therapy, coaching, and wellness retreats to recover from the stress of a poorly chosen environment. *A more strategic relocation can often solve what expensive coping mechanisms merely soothe.*

The same principle applies to work style. The highest paying job is not always the most valuable one, especially when measured in terms of autonomy, energy, and sustainability. A slightly lower-paying role with flexible hours may open space for health, creativity, or side income. A part-time job in a values-aligned organisation may be more fulfilling than a high-status corporate role that demands identity sacrifice. Remote work may unlock geographic options that reshape your cost of living entirely. These are not indulgent considerations. They are rational optimisations—because *money that preserves well-being goes further than money that constantly compensates for its own costs.*

Community, too, is often treated as an accidental by-product of circumstance—who happens to live nearby, who's still around from university, who works in your field. But relationships are infrastructure. They either compound or erode your financial and emotional resilience. A strong, generous, practical community can lower costs, increase trust, and multiply your optionality. Co-living arrangements, shared childcare, collaborative projects, knowledge exchange—all of these are forms of wealth that don't show up on spreadsheets but materially impact quality of life. *A low-budget life surrounded by intelligent, trustworthy, energising people will outperform a high-budget life lived in social isolation.*

Consumption habits reveal the most about what kind of lifestyle you're actually designing. Every purchase is a vote—not just for a product, but for a rhythm of life. When people say they "can't afford" lifestyle design, they often mean they're unwilling to shift what they already consume. But intentional living requires active divestment. That may mean buying less but better. It may mean rejecting subscription creep. It may mean replacing dopamine-chasing impulse buys with investments in skills or experiences. *Design is not about adding—it's about curating.*

Many people believe frugality is about deprivation. But strategic frugality is better understood as *deliberate exclusion.* It's the discipline of narrowing inputs to protect space for the things that matter most. For example, someone earning a modest salary who commits to living car-free may unlock more financial freedom than someone who earns double but drives an expensive vehicle to a high-stress office daily. Lifestyle design is less about *what* you can afford, and more about *what you're willing to stop paying for.*

Of course, none of this means ignoring real constraints. There are situations—housing insecurity, chronic illness, caregiving obligations—where options genuinely shrink. But even within constraint, agency is not erased. The question becomes: *What variables can I influence?* What assumptions am I making that could be challenged? Could I move laterally into a similar role with better conditions? Could I design a home routine that reduces stress? Could I borrow, barter, or build what I can't buy? Lifestyle design on a budget requires reframing: from consumer to creator, from participant to architect.

There's a cultural myth that says design begins with abundance. But in practice, it is often born from discontent. Many great lives began with someone saying: *this can't be it.* They didn't wait for permission. They used whatever resources they had—spare time, quiet mornings, overlooked spaces—to build something better. They asked unpopular questions, such as: What if I worked less but created more? What if I made £5,000 less but needed £10,000 less? What if I took a risk now, while the stakes are still small?

One of the smartest strategies for lifestyle design on a budget is to prototype. Don't overhaul everything at once. Instead, run low-cost experiments. Try living in a different area for a month. Work remotely for a week from a co-living space. Try a four-day workweek, even informally. Declutter your wardrobe and notice what changes emotionally. Set strict constraints—no takeaways for a month, no social media after 6 p.m.—and track what happens to your energy. These micro-tests cost little but reveal much. *They move you from theory to texture—from aspiration to embodiment.*

Another overlooked strategy is substitution. Instead of trying to "afford" what others have, you redesign the frame entirely. You don't need a luxury gym when you have a community run club. You don't need expensive travel if your local life is filled with wonder. You don't need fine dining when you cook intentionally with friends. *The real lifestyle flex is not consumption—it's authorship.* It's being the person who shapes their days with care, not just fills them with distractions.

And finally, it's essential to acknowledge the emotional dimension. Lifestyle design can provoke resistance—internal and external. You may face envy, misunderstanding, or even subtle sabotage from people invested in more conventional paths. You may feel guilt for wanting ease before you've earned it, or shame for not pursuing prestige. These are not signs to stop. They are signs you're doing something original. *Lifestyle design on a budget is not about retreating from ambition—it's about refusing to mortgage your joy for delayed promises.*

You are not designing in spite of your financial limits—you're designing because of them. Scarcity is not always a barrier. Sometimes it's a filter. It forces you to notice what matters, discard what doesn't, and lay foundations that will support you when more resources eventually arrive. A life shaped in this way becomes not just more affordable—but more antifragile, more distinct, and more deeply yours.

The Power of Long Bets:

Modern culture incentivises immediacy. We're trained to optimise for the short term: quick wins, rapid returns, visible validation. Patience is rarely framed as a strategic asset. Yet across almost every field—finance, art, science, health, relationships—the most profound transformations accrue not from intensity, but duration. *The most valuable outcomes are often those that take the longest to materialise—and the longest to appreciate.*

Long bets are deliberate choices to pursue actions, projects, or paths that may appear inefficient or irrational in the short term but are deeply aligned with one's values and vision. They are, by design, unsexy. They resist applause. They often require you to delay gratification, withstand doubt, and hold a line that only makes sense in retrospect. Yet this very quality is what makes them powerful. *When you bet long, you shift from performative urgency to grounded conviction.*

Consider a young professional who decides to invest a few hours each week learning a second language, without an immediate need or use case. Years later, that skill enables them to negotiate an international role, build cross-border relationships, or access foreign markets others can't. Or take the example of someone who begins writing consistently online—not to go viral, but to clarify their thinking. Over time, they build a body of work that attracts unseen opportunities, invitations, and partnerships. These aren't overnight successes. They are compounding advantages seeded by intention and watered with patience.

In a world that fetishises optionality, long bets look like constraints. Committing to a path for years can feel risky when you're told to "keep your options open." But the paradox is that *long-term commitment often unlocks more freedom than constant pivoting.* When you go deep, not wide, you develop rare insights, hone durable skills, and cultivate trust. People begin to associate your name with something distinctive. You stop being interchangeable. The risk of commitment becomes its own insurance policy.

Long bets can take many forms. Choosing a career path that matches your internal rhythm, rather than market trends. Building a financial portfolio around low-fee, diversified index funds instead of trying to time the next meme stock. Opting for a simpler lifestyle that allows for greater creative freedom. Raising children with consistent, intentional values instead of chasing elite enrichment. Writing a book that may sell modestly now, but shapes how people think for decades. *The unifying thread is orientation: choosing what endures over what excites.*

This mindset is not romanticism. It's resilience. Long bets force you to decouple your identity from external rewards. They ask: *Can I continue even when nobody's watching?* They inoculate you against the volatility of markets, moods, and social approval. This is not to say you ignore feedback. It means you calibrate to a deeper internal compass, rather than the noise of the moment. In doing so, you build both vision and durability—two traits increasingly rare in a distracted economy.

What often deters people from making long bets is uncertainty. "What if I choose wrong?" But that question assumes there is one perfect bet, one flawless outcome. The better question is: *What kind of problems am I willing to face for the next decade?* A long bet is not about eliminating difficulty—it's about selecting your struggle. A meaningful pursuit will not be frictionless. But it will be coherent. When setbacks arise—as they always do—your response won't be to abandon the field, but to adapt within a path that still feels right.

Financially, long bets take on tangible form. Instead of chasing speculative gains, you build a portfolio designed for slow, sustainable growth. Instead of spending aggressively in your 20s to project an image, you live below your means to buy flexibility in your 30s. You contribute consistently to retirement accounts, even when it's boring. You invest in skills with no immediate payoff—coding, public speaking, negotiation—because you know they compound. *You shift from consuming status to accumulating leverage.*

Psychologically, long bets foster identity coherence. When your actions align with a long-term narrative, your choices feel less random. You don't need to ask "what should I do next?" every month. You have a scaffolding. That scaffolding may evolve, but it offers orientation in a chaotic world. You start to see setbacks not as existential threats, but as part of the arc. You don't crumble every time a door closes—because your game is bigger than this month's metrics.

Critically, long bets are not just individual. They are relational. Deciding to nurture a marriage for decades instead of seeking novelty. Building a community project that might take years to blossom. Mentoring others without the expectation of immediate return. These investments often produce the most profound forms of wealth—trust, meaning, loyalty, and a sense of legacy. *Short-termism erodes relationships. Long bets fortify them.*

The challenge, of course, is maintaining faith without immediate feedback. In the early stages, long bets feel like labouring in the dark. You can't show your progress on a dashboard. You don't get "likes" for persistence. This is where most people give up. The trick is to build internal feedback loops. Notice micro-movements. Track your consistency. Celebrate the process, not just the result. Share your thinking in public—not to get validation, but to stay honest. *Trust that the future belongs to those willing to be underestimated while they build.*

Long bets also cultivate emotional antifragility. When your goals are spaced over years, you become less reactive. You stop chasing every trend or fearing every dip. You start thinking in decades, not quarters. This breeds calm—not from passivity, but from perspective. *You're not here to win the sprint. You're here to build the track.*

Yet, not every long bet has to be heavy or heroic. It could be choosing to learn an instrument in your spare time. Committing to writing a weekly newsletter. Growing your own vegetables. Learning how to cook well. These are small decisions with outsize impact over time. They add texture, joy, and depth to life. They remind you that you are not just surviving—you are *composing* a life.

Importantly, a long bet is not a rigid plan. It's a directional wager. You may shift course, refine tactics, or discover a better destination. But the point is not perfection. It's momentum. You are building something bigger than the present. You are resisting the erosion of attention, depth, and conviction. You are making peace with being a beginner, with going unnoticed, with failing quietly before succeeding publicly.

As with investing, the earlier you start placing long bets, the more options you'll have later. But it's never too late to begin. Every long bet you place—on yourself, your relationships, your work, your vision—becomes a signal to your future self: *I trust you to carry this forward.* That trust, sustained over time, becomes confidence. And confidence, earned through years of alignment, is one of the rarest and most valuable assets you can hold.

Let others optimise for what's visible, what's fast, what's trending. You're playing a different game. You're building a different life. Not louder—but deeper. Not sooner—but truer. *The power of long bets is not that they guarantee success—but that they make success, when it comes, deeply earned and unmistakably yours.*

Freedom Beyond the Algorithm:

There is a quiet but growing cost to living by algorithms. It is not merely the commodification of attention or the erosion of privacy—it is the gradual outsourcing of decision-making itself. What to buy, who to follow, where to live, how to spend your time—these are no longer choices developed in solitude or crafted from first principles. They are increasingly pre-solved for you by machines optimised not for your wellbeing, but for your predictability. *The more data-driven your life becomes, the more pre-scripted it risks becoming. And what's sold as convenience often operates as constraint.*

True wealth, as this book argues, is not just financial—it's the ability to direct your life with clarity and sovereignty. Yet that capacity is quietly under siege. Most people do not consciously mimic mainstream financial behaviours, career paths, or lifestyle patterns. They absorb them ambiently, by scrolling. *To escape poverty is hard. But to escape imitation may be even harder—because the latter does not feel like a trap. It feels like belonging.*

What we're confronting here is not just the algorithmic influence of platforms like TikTok, YouTube, or Instagram. It's a broader culture of conformity masquerading as freedom. When every financial planner recommends the same five asset classes, when every productivity guru hawks the same digital routines, when every influencer's version of luxury looks eerily similar—*the room for original design shrinks*. Even abundance can become performative if it's defined externally.

To live freely, then, requires more than rejecting noise. It means cultivating the inner resolve to define success on your own terms—even when that definition earns you less applause, slower progress, or fewer likes. It means understanding that *authentic wealth doesn't scale like content.* The deeper your alignment, the more invisible your path may appear to others.

Consider the case of someone who chooses part-time work not out of necessity, but as a strategic decision to buy time for creative pursuits. On paper, their income may appear modest; in reality, they're operating from a higher level of self-authorship. Or the person who opts out of property ownership in favour of geographic freedom, resisting the societal script that equates mortgages with maturity. Or the couple that chooses to rent a modest home near community and walkability, prioritising relational capital over square footage. *Each of these choices subverts algorithmic norms by foregrounding values over optics.*

Freedom in this context is not about detachment from tools or tech. It is about *disentanglement from default narratives.* The algorithm is not evil. It is indifferent. Its only job is to keep you engaged. It cannot help you choose well, only predictably. It will not reward integrity, only consistency. The burden, then, is on the individual to opt out consciously—not of technology, but of unexamined templates.

This is particularly relevant in personal finance. Every year, thousands of young adults enter the workforce and immediately lock themselves into life paths shaped more by proximity than intentionality. They pick careers based on income rankings, not interest. They rent flats based on TikTok aesthetics, not life rhythm. They save and invest with vague goals—retire early, buy property, "build wealth"—but little internal clarity. *When algorithms shape both aspiration and behaviour, the person loses authorship while believing they are choosing freely.*

The antidote is not rebellion but design. Begin by interrogating what you want life to feel like—not look like on a profile. What time of day do you want to wake up? What kind of conversations replenish you? What pace of life suits your nervous system? What activities make you forget to check your phone? These are not aesthetic questions—they are existential ones. They force you to shift from simulation to substance.

There's a reason intentional living often looks less impressive on the surface. It's quieter, slower, sometimes leaner. It does not announce itself through curated highlight reels. But it delivers something rare in our time: *an intact sense of self.* When your calendar reflects your real priorities, when your bank account supports your real values, when your living space is built for actual joy rather than perceived prestige—*you are free, even if you earn less than the median influencer.*

This does not mean you ignore metrics. It means you *use them, but refuse to be defined by them.* Your income matters—but not more than your autonomy. Your visibility matters—but not more than your privacy. Your reputation matters—but not more than your integrity. These trade-offs cannot be resolved by spreadsheet logic alone. They require reflection, solitude, and often, the courage to disappoint the culture you were raised in.

One of the quiet revolutions happening today is the reclamation of agency through micro-decisions. Choosing not to check your phone before breakfast. Saying no to offers that promise scale but compromise substance. Refusing to anchor your self-worth in engagement numbers. Taking a social media break not to "detox," but to design. These acts are small but cumulative. *They form a discipline of self-authorship.*

From a financial lens, this also means crafting wealth plans that support your life rather than overshadow it. Not every portfolio needs to optimise for maximum growth. Some are built for stability, others for freedom, others still for creative risk. The point is not to mimic high performers, but to engineer a system that *lets you live well now and sustainably later.* Your goals may be modest, your means lean, but if your design is true, *you will experience a kind of peace that no trending algorithm can generate.*

The broader cultural narrative will always promote more—more efficiency, more reach, more income, more "impact." But *the deeper work is to ask what is enough.* And once you define it, *to protect it fiercely.* To say no, not because you lack ambition, but because your ambition has matured. To step away, not because you failed, but because the game stopped being worth playing. These are not acts of quitting—they are acts of sovereignty.

As this book nears its close, the final message is this: the truest form of wealth is not passive income or financial independence. It is *the power to shape your life from the inside out.* To make decisions that reflect not what is trending, but what is true. To live in a way that *feels yours*, even if it's misunderstood. To escape not just scarcity, but imitation. That is freedom beyond the algorithm. And that is what makes everything else worth building.

Conclusion

If you've made it this far, something within you has shifted—and that shift matters more than any bank balance. While this book has often spoken of money, its true concern has never been accumulation. It has been agency. Clarity. The quiet power of self-authorship. The transition from surviving a system to consciously shaping your place within it. The £100,000 figure was never the point; it was the pretext, a tangible milestone to anchor something far less measurable but profoundly more significant: a new lens through which to view yourself in the world.

Money is tangible. It appears in statements, transactions, projections. But the change you've undergone is subtler. It shows in those moments when you pause before spending and ask, "Does this reflect who I am becoming?" When boundaries are set not merely to protect your budget, but to safeguard your peace. When intention trumps impulse. These are not mere behaviours; they are markers of identity. They declare: I am no longer reacting to money. I am relating to it—with composure, curiosity, and discernment.

This book has sought to restore not only skills, but a sense of authorship. Early experiences with money are often passive, fraught with scarcity, shame, or inherited scripts. The default is reaction: chasing, comparing, fearing. By contrast, the reader who reaches this chapter has paused, observed patterns, rewritten assumptions, and anchored goals in values rather than noise. They are beginning to convert a financial life into a designed life—and that matters more than compound interest ever could.

This chapter is not a summary; it is a zoomed-out perspective, an opportunity to witness the trajectory you've chosen. You have not merely earned, saved, or invested. You have made choices aligned with your principles. You have said no to urgency. You have practised clarity in a culture that profits from distraction. That clarity is a discipline, not a one-off victory—and like all disciplines, it grows through repetition, not intensity.

Setbacks will occur, of course. Financial life rarely proceeds in straight lines. Markets fluctuate. Needs shift. Life introduces uninvited variables. But these no longer threaten you. You are no longer anchored to the illusion of control; you are anchored to discernment. You know when to pause, when to adapt, when to return to principles—even after a detour. That is what makes progress irreversible.

There comes a moment for many readers—somewhere between practical exercises and mindset rewiring—when the desire to outsource financial thinking fades. The search for the "right hack" diminishes. Confidence emerges from congruence, not competence alone. You begin to trust your capacity to think systemically, choose deliberately, and tolerate ambiguity. This is the inflection point. You now possess a frame, a compass, a language. The tools serve you rather than overwhelm you.

Consider what has changed. Money, once synonymous with pressure, now connotes possibility. Impulsive spending, controlling saving, avoidance—these reflexes give way to pause, inquiry, and long-term perspective. Fragmented tactics become integrated thinking. Leverage is mapped, fears tested, busyness dismantled, lopsided habits transformed into coherent systems. You are no longer the subject of your financial narrative; you are the author.

This authorship extends beyond the next milestone. Whether you reach £200,000 or £2 million, scale a business or maintain a steady solo practice, the underlying work remains the same: living in alignment with values rather than validation metrics. It may mean building slowly, earning less than possible to preserve autonomy, redefining growth as depth rather than breadth. These are not compromises—they are discernment. They mark someone who knows how they want their life to feel, not merely what it funds.

In a culture obsessed with accumulation, alignment is rare. It is easier to broadcast a six-figure income than to live a six-figure life of coherence, patience, and purpose. Yet this book has never been about impressiveness; it is about wholeness. Achievement with coherence. You are wealthier not merely because net worth has risen, but because decisions are cleaner, stress lower, and days feel more yours.

This does not imply perfection. Financial adulthood is not a destination, but a posture. Rooted not in flawless execution, but in owning choices with self-respect and humility. Mistakes will happen, but they are no longer character indictments. Your bank balance is no longer a stand-in for self-worth. You have decoupled identity from the market's verdict.

The £100,000 milestone may be ahead, or behind. Either way, the true victory lies in what it demonstrated: you can construct a financial life without abandoning yourself. Pragmatism and principle coexist. You can earn without overextending, save without hoarding, invest without forsaking values. Growth is no longer about arbitrary benchmarks—it is about expanding capacity for choice, generosity, and peace.

As you close this book, seek not the next step, but the next questions. How will you maintain clarity under pressure? What must be protected as options multiply? Who do you wish to become as opportunity expands? These are not mere financial queries—they are design questions. And now, you are equipped to answer them deliberately rather than reactively.

Books, advice, frameworks—they will come and go. What remains is sturdier: a philosophy, a blueprint for thinking, choosing, and relating to money as a tool rather than a tyrant. That is the lasting transformation. You have built not only assets, but authorship. From here forward, the script is yours to write.

You've Changed More Than Your Net Worth:

There's a subtle but seismic moment when a person realises that wealth is not merely about what they own—it's about how they see. By the time you've reached this part of the book, the more important growth isn't in your account balance. It's in your perception. Of money. Of self. Of power. The shift is internal and irreversible: *you no longer move through the world as someone waiting for permission*. You act from clarity, not compliance. From purpose, not pressure. The £100,000 was never the goal—it was the evidence. The visible trace of an invisible transformation.

You don't build lasting financial autonomy by memorising tips or mimicking someone else's playbook. You build it by changing the way you relate to decisions. When you began this book, your choices may have felt scattered or reactionary—driven by fear, confusion, or the sheer volume of noise surrounding modern finance. Now, if you've done the work, your choices carry a different weight. They are anchored. They are slower but more resolute. You're no longer trying to win the game as it's been handed to you. You're questioning the rules, rewriting the stakes, and—most critically—*choosing with authorship.*

This is not self-help gloss. It's behavioural architecture. What's changed is not just your financial plan, but the mental and emotional scaffolding that surrounds it. You've trained yourself to pause before the automatic yes or no. You've examined inherited scripts that once masqueraded as common sense. You've learned to see through lifestyle inflation, the hustle narrative, the false idol of perpetual optimisation. You've practised discernment—not in theory, but in context. And *that discernment is your real asset.*

There's a reason so many people hit financial milestones and still feel hollow: they never changed the story. They followed strategies without shifting identity. They "won" the game but stayed psychologically shackled to fear, shame, or scarcity. But you, if you've absorbed this book as intended, have altered the foundation. Your wealth is no longer the sum of your assets. It's the strength of your alignment.

It's easy to focus on external results: the first investment account, the growing emergency fund, the automation system that hums in the background. These matter. But what truly marks your evolution is the change in who you trust—*yourself.* Not blindly. Not with bravado. But with grounded, earned confidence. The kind that comes from testing your assumptions, confronting your financial anxieties, and finding you didn't collapse under the weight. The kind that says: "I can navigate uncertainty. I can adjust without unraveling. I can lead my financial life without outsourcing my values."

What this chapter offers is not a final word but a wider lens. We zoom out, not to detach, but to integrate. To see the entire arc: how you moved from avoidance to engagement, from fragmentation to coherence. You're no longer building wealth on someone else's timeline. You're defining what a meaningful life looks like—*and letting your money serve that vision, not sabotage it.*

Many people are taught to see money as either security or status. Few are taught to see it as stewardship. You've now stepped into that mindset. You don't hoard. You don't chase. You cultivate. You deploy. You take responsibility for your energy, your influence, your impact. That shift—from passive recipient to active designer—is not a mindset hack. It's an identity recalibration. One that affects everything from how you negotiate a salary to how you spend a Sunday.

Importantly, this change has been earned. You didn't just read about financial frameworks—you implemented them. You felt the resistance, the fear of missing out, the discomfort of delayed gratification. You made trade-offs. You said no to urgency. You stayed with the discomfort of simplicity. And slowly, methodically, *you reclaimed your agency*. No book can do that for you. That's yours.

What happens next? More choices. More noise. More tests of integrity. But now you approach those decisions differently. You're not overwhelmed by complexity. You break it down. You ask better questions. You don't just seek efficiency—you seek alignment. And when things go sideways—as they inevitably will—you return to the foundation, not with self-blame, but with awareness. You are no longer fragile.

This work doesn't end. The financial world will keep shifting. Markets will wobble. Careers will pivot. Needs will change. But your centre will hold, because it's been shaped by something deeper than strategies—it's been shaped by values. The old paradigm said: earn more, spend less, be smart. The new paradigm, the one you've internalised, says: *live intentionally, choose coherently, honour your limits and desires without shame*. That's what it means to become sovereign.

And sovereignty is not perfection. It's authorship under pressure. It's holding complexity with calm. It's saying: "I may not control the economy, but I control how I move through it." That's a profound transformation. One that reaches far beyond the spreadsheet. One that cannot be undone by market fluctuations or fleeting comparisons.

You are now someone who listens before reacting. Who invests with purpose, not just returns. Who asks not just what a purchase costs, but what it costs emotionally, energetically, ethically. You are not flawless, but you are awake. And that alone sets you apart.

As this book closes, it doesn't hand you a roadmap. It hands you the pen. The external benchmarks—£100k, the career milestones, the polished "success stories"—were never the point. They were practice fields. They gave you the terrain to test and refine something infinitely more durable: your discernment, your authorship, your commitment to a life that reflects who you truly are.

The path ahead will not be linear. You will forget, falter, revise. That's not failure. That's the texture of real life. But with each cycle, you will return to this truth: *You are not here to mimic wealth. You are here to design it—on your terms, in your voice, with your values at the centre.*

And that, more than any figure in your bank account, is the legacy of this work.

About the Author

Julian Raye writes at the intersection of money, meaning, and modern life. Blending real-world experience with a deep sensitivity to the emotional and psychological sides of personal finance, Julian helps a new generation rewrite their financial story—without the shame, jargon, or burnout. His mission is to make wealth feel human again: less about spreadsheets and status, and more about power, permission, and presence. When he's not writing, he's listening—closely—to the quiet fears and bold dreams that shape how people move through money and move toward themselves.

www.ingramcontent.com/pod-product-compliance
Lightning Source LLC
Chambersburg PA
CBHW031349230926
51848CB00002B/446